백 투 　 **BACK TO**
더 퓨처 **THE FUTURE**

백 투   BACK TO
더 퓨처 THE FUTURE

한국 현대미술의 동시대성 탐험기
AN EXPLORATION OF CONTEMPORANEITY
IN KOREAN CONTEMPORARY ART

목차

Contents

발간사

《백 투 더 퓨처: 한국 현대미술의 동시대성 탐험기》(이하 《백 투 더 퓨처》)는
국립현대미술관이 지난 5년 동안 수집한 작품들을 들여다보면서 주목해야 할
지점들을 포착하고 이를 분석하여 기획한 특별전입니다. 미술관의 작품 수집
정책과 방향에 따라 매년 시기·장르·주제별로 고른 수집 분포를 보이는바,
미술관은 2018년부터 2022년까지 다양한 시기·장르·주제의 작품을 모았습니다.
그 가운데 공성훈, 김범, 박이소 등을 비롯하여 1990년대라는 대내외적으로 급격한
변화의 시대에 예술적 토대를 딛고 있는, 소위 한국 현대미술의 동시대성을 보여주는
작품들이 이 시기에 집중적으로 다수 수집되었다는 특징을 살펴볼 수 있습니다.

《백 투 더 퓨처》는 1980년대 후반부터 대략 2010년대까지를 시대적
상호 영향 범위 안에 두고, 1990년대 초 활발한 활동을 전개한 작가들의 당시
작업과 최근으로 이어진 작업을 선보였고, 20세기 말에서 21세기 초, 소위 Y2K를
경험하고 성장하여 지금 우리 동시대 미술 현장의 주요 작가로 위치하고 있는
작가의 작품도 전시하였습니다. 그런가 하면 이들의 작업을 통해서 확인되는
한국 현대미술의 동시대적 양상 속에서 살펴봐야 할 또 다른 세대 작가의 작품도
볼 기회를 마련하였습니다. 한국 현대미술의 동시대성이 형성된 맥락과
그 흐름을 이어 보여주는 작품들에 대한 수집은 지속적으로 진행해야 할 부분이고,
이번 전시에서는 그리 멀지 않은 과거이지만 역사화가 전개되어야 하는 시기의
우리 현대미술을 확인하는 기회를 갖고자 하였습니다.

이번 《백 투 더 퓨처》 전시를 위하여 도움을 주신 분들, 도록 집필자 분들,
그리고 의미 있는 전시를 위해 노력을 아끼지 않은 미술관 직원들에게
감사의 말씀을 드립니다.

박종달
국립현대미술관 관장 직무대리

Preface

Back to the Future: An Exploration of Contemporaneity of Korean Contemporary Art is an exhibition organized with the intention of sharing artwork from the collection of the National Museum of Modern and Contemporary Art, Korea (MMCA) with the public. Covering artworks acquired by the museum over a five-year period, from 2018 to 2022, the exhibition thoroughly examines the characteristics of noteworthy acquisitions from this time. In accordance with MMCA acquisition policies and directions, the artwork acquired each year has shown an even distribution in terms of era, genre, and theme with pieces acquired over the recent five-years being no exception. One of the most important characteristics observed in these particular acquisitions is that a large number of works are from the artists who demonstrate the contemporaneity of Korean contemporary art, based on the transitional historical period of the 1990s, including figures such as Kong Sunghun, Kim Beom, and Bahc Yiso.

While the chronological emphasis may be on the 1990s, the exhibition includes works ranging from the late 1980s to 2010 in its scope of influence; in doing so, it hopes to highlight the time in which many of the featured artists were establishing their artistic identity—between the late 1980s and early 1990s—along with some of their more recent artistic activities. Also presented among the museum's acquisitions are works by artists who grew up amid a climate, in the late 20th and early 21st centuries, that saw the intersection and coexistence of analog and digital. Later emerging in the scene, they have since established themselves as important presences in the Korean contemporary art world. Furthermore, the exhibition seeks to provide viewers with the opportunity to observe works by artists who, back then, contributed notably to the creation of the context behind the contemporaneity of Korean contemporary art; this is evident in works created by currently practicing artists in the present day. Major artworks from this period are still being added to the museum's collection, and while it is impossible to show all previously acquired works here, the exhibition, through the selected artists and artworks, offers a chance to reexamine Korean art during a period that, while belonging to the not-too-distant past, still warrants being historicized.

My sincere gratitude goes out to all the people who helped for this exhibition, the writers who contributed catalog, and the museum staff who spared no effort in preparing for this exhibition.

Park Jongdal
Acting Director, National Museum of Modern and Contemporary Art, Korea

백 투 더 퓨처:
한국 현대미술의
동시대성
탐험기

김형미

국립현대미술관 학예연구사

≪백 투 더 퓨처: 한국 현대미술의 동시대성 탐험기≫는 국립현대미술관 소장품을 중심으로 기획한 특별전으로, 2018년부터 2022년까지 지난 5년 동안 미술관이 수집한 작품들을 살펴보면서 주목할 만한 특징을 확인하고 이를 집중적으로 들여다보았다. 이 시기 눈에 띄는 지점은 공성훈, 김범, 박이소 등을 포함, 1990년대라는 시대전환기를 예술적 토양으로 삼아 소위 한국 현대미술의 동시대적 양상을 드러낸 작가들의 작품이 다수 수집되었다는 것이다. 이에 시기적으로 1990년대를 중심으로 1980년대 후반부터 2010년대까지를 상호 영향 범위로 설정하고, 1980년대 말 1990년대 초 작가적 정체성을 구축한 작가들의 당시 작업과 최근으로 이어진 그들의 작품 활동을 살펴보고자 했다. 그런가 하면 20세기 말, 21세기 초 아날로그와 디지털이 교차·혼재하던 시기를 관통하며 성장하고, 한국 미술 현장에 등장하여 지금 우리 현대미술계 주요 작가로 자리매김한 작가들의 작품들도 선보였다. 또한 그들의 작품을 통해서 확인되고 지금도 이어지고 있는 한국 현대미술의 동시대성의 맥락 속에서 주목할 작가들의 작품도 마주하는 기회를 제공하고자 했다. 해당 시기 주요 작품들에 대한 수집은 여전히 진행 중이고, 관련해서 이미 수집된 소장품을 모두 이 자리에서 소개할 수는 없는 여건이나 이번 전시를 통해 그리 멀지 않은 과거이지만 역사화의 단계로 조속히 유입되어야 하는 시기의 한국미술을 새삼 확인하는 계기를 마련하고자 했다.

'백 투 더 퓨처'

전시명 '백 투 더 퓨처'는 1985년 개봉한 할리우드 영화「백 투 더 퓨처」(Back to the Future)와 동명이다. 영화 속 주인공 마티는 1985년을 기점으로 타임머신을 타고 30년 전후로 시간여행을 한다. 과거-현재-미래를 이동하며 주인공은 복잡다단한 상황에 얽히고설킨다. 다소 선형적인 전개 방식이긴 하나 시공간이 충돌하는 이야기를 담은 이 영화가 국내에 개봉된 1987년은 한국 현대미술의 동시대성의 맥락이 형성되기 시작한 때로 종종 거론되는 시기이다. 1980년대 말부터 1990년대는 대내외적으로 급변하는 정치·사회·경제적 상황만큼이나 영화, 음악, 만화 등 대중문화예술이 당시 새로운 세대에게 더없이 큰 영향력을 가진 때였다. 시대 변환과 맞물려 전개된 전향적 세대 전환은 이 시기의 가장 핵심적인 변화라 할 수 있다. 기존 관습이 묻어나지 않고, 이전 논리로는 해석되지 않는 현상과 상황을 거리낌 없이 타고 넘는 세대의 탄생은 해당 시기를 정의하는 주요 기제이다. 미래로의 소환·호출(Back to the Future)에서 미래를 '지금'이라 놓고 볼 때, 지금 여기로 소환된 것이 무엇인지는 그 복잡다단한 통로를 걷다 보면 만날 수 있을 것이다.

시대 변환과 미술 지형 변동

간략하게 1990년대 전후 국내외 상황을 들여다 보자면, 우리 내부적으로는 1987년 6월항쟁, 1986년 아시안게임, 1988년 서울올림픽, 그리고 1993년 문민정부의 출현을 통해 절차적 차원의 민주주의 성숙이 연이어 전개되었고, 이를 토대로 경제 성장과 세계화 전략의 추진 등 이전과는 다른 사회적 기제들이 작동하고 실제 삶의 변화에 영향을 미치고 있었다. 그런가 하면 1980년대 말에서 1990년대 초로 이어지는 시기는 전례없이 세계사의 차원에서 커다란 변혁이 일어난 때이다. 1989년 베를린장벽이 붕괴되었고, 동유럽의 사회주의 체제 또한 붕괴와 변혁을 맞이하는가 하면, 1991년에는 구 소련이 해체함으로써 결과적으로 냉전의 시대가 막을 내렸다. 이에 세계 질서는 정치가 아닌 경제 중심의 자본 논리가 지배하는 상황으로 전개되었다. 그런 와중에 우리 사회는 유례없는 압축성장 이후 국가적 재난 차원의 IMF 경제위기를 맞이했고, 또한 이를 극복하는 과정을 겪었으며, 이를 통해 우리 사회를 버텨내고 지키는 근본적인 원동력에 대해서 각성하게 되었다. 1990년대 이후 글로벌리즘 시대 우리가 공유한 세계 내 보편성이라는 가치는 결과적으로 오랜 세월 우리 사회 내 다수의 노력과 희생을 통해 얻은 것임을 확인하였고, 더불어 1990년대 사회적, 경제적 변화와 확장 못지 않게 이어졌던 사건·사고의 충격은 당대를 관통하며 지나온 세대들에게 스며있을 또 다른 시대적 흔적이었다.[1]

1990년대 이후 문화예술의 흐름을 이해할 수 있게 하는 특징 중 하나로 정보통신기술의 혁신과 소비문화의 확산을 들 수 있다. 인터넷 등 정보통신과학기술의 혁신, 그리고 소위 '전 지구적' 차원에서 가능한 동시적 연결이 가속화하면서 1990년대에서 2000년대로 이어지는 우리 미술계도 관련한 변화 기류를 맞이했다. 그 중심에 당대 새롭게 떠오른 세대가 자리하고 있었다. 유동하고 정체되기를 거부하는 당대 문화는 1990년대 후반 급속히 상용화한 인터넷 환경에 의해, 그리고 이를 거침없이 활용하는 세대를 통해 빠르게 확산되었다.

최근 대중문화예술이 재소환해 유행을 타고 있는 소위 '1990년대 스타일'은 당시 치열한 시대 변환을 통해 확인하고 획득한 사회문화적 토대와 실천들을 떠올리게 한다. 1990년대를 관통하여 2000년대로 이어지는 이 시기의 미술은 마치 지각변동과도 같은 전 세계적 체질 변화 상황과 이와 연관된 한국의 사회 환경을 그대로 흡수했다. 그래서 동시대 한국 현대미술은 보편적이면서 특정적이고, 전 세계적인 차원과 우리 사회 내적 맥락을 함께 고려할 때 제대로 이해할 수 있다. '동시대성'은 상황과 사태를 순차적이고 선형적인 시공간의 흐름으로 다루거나

---

1 정헌이, 「미술」, 한국예술종합학교
한국예술연구소 엮음,
『한국현대예술사대계 VI-1990년대』
(서울: 시공사, 2005), 269–270.

인식하는 체계와는 다른 접근을 가능하게 하는 것으로, 복합적이고 뒤얽힌 시공간과 상황, 조건들을 수용하는 판단 가치와 관련되어 있다. 이와 같은 관점의 바탕이 되는 맥락을 당대 발현된 미술 행위들에서 확인하고자 했다. 이에 이번 전시의 시작점에서 우선 공성훈, 김범, 박이소, 이동기, 이용백, 최정화, 서현석 등의 작품을 통해 한국 현대미술의 동시대적 양상의 형성이 의미하는 바를 살펴보고자 했다.

이질성과 그 비평적 시공간

1980년대 후반에서 1990년대까지 우리는 대내외적으로 급격한 사회변화를 맞이했다. 이는 한국 현대미술의 동시대성을 확보하는 토양을 확실하게 다져냈다. 1990년대 우리 사회는 지난 시기의 급격한 산업화와 근대화를 통한 고도성장의 수혜와 폐해가 교차 충돌하고 있었다. 그리고 전근대와 근대가 해결하지 못한 난제들을 품은 상태에서 근대 '이후'를 맞이하여 서로 다른 시간들이 혼재된 상황을 겪어야 했다. 이에 더해 세계화와 신자유주의의 거센 유입도 있었다. 혼돈과 새로움의 역동 속에서 우리 사회는 오히려 명증해진 지정학적, 역사적 현실을 마주하게 되었다. 이번 전시에는 이 시기를 관통하여 성장하며 창작 역량을 구축한 작가들이 포진해 있다. 그야말로 동시대 미술 작가라 명명할 수 있는 이들은 장르와 영역 사이의 관습적 구분에 갇히지 않고, 국내외 변화 흐름을 재빨리 간파하며, 다르게 전개된 경제사회적 조건과 상황을 전략적으로 활용할 줄 알았고, 대중문화사회적 환경을 거침없이 받아들이는 등 복잡다단한 현실의 관계망을 기꺼이 타고 넘나들었다.

우리 미술계 내부의 변화도 이 시기 빼놓을 수 없는 주요 현상이었다. 우선 외적인 변화를 보면, 다수의 주요 국공립 미술관이 설립되었고, 대안공간들이 생겨났으며, 다수의 국제미술행사들이 개최되는가 하면, 미술시장도 다변화하였고, 온오프라인을 넘나들며 잡지 등을 포함한 미술관련 매체들이 생겨났다. 말하자면, 적어도 우리 현대미술이 세계 동시대 미술 현장과 인프라 차원에서 그 보조를 맞추는 데에는 크게 문제가 없음을 의미했다. 상당히 긴 시간 우리 현대미술계는 세계미술계 내 인정과 편입에 대한 조급함이 자리해 있었다. 글로벌 시대 우리나라를 포함한 비서구권 미술은 비엔날레와 같은 대규모 국제미술행사를 통해 세계미술계와의 접촉을 유지해 나갔다. 이러한 국제미술행사들이 세계미술계 내 편입에 대한 강박을 어느 정도 해소하는 역할을 했다고 볼 수 있다. 그러나 동질화 등 근본적인 문제들은 여전히 남아 있다. 그래서 대형 국제미술행사에 참여했다는 것이 마치 동시대성을 획득한 것으로 읽어내는 단선적인 이해와 평가는 '동시대성'과 관련한 이질적이고 복합적 관계망, 그리고 그 관계망 속에서 나오는 수많은 다층적 발화들을 읽어내지 못한 결과라 하겠다.

이번 전시에 소개된 작가들의 미술행위는 글로벌리즘 시대 내 세계 미술계와의 보편성 공유와 조형어휘의 동질성이라는 표면적 차원과 별개로, 빠르게 변모하는 시대 상황과 이에 따른 이질적 혼종이라는 자생적 토양을 품고 이를 개별적으로 발화시킨 결과로 볼 수 있다. 2000년대 초 본격화되는 우리 동시대 미술 구도 속에서 개별적 정체성을 발현하고 지금까지 그 작업역량을 보여주고 있는 작가들의 작품을 통해 긴 세월 우리 미술이 맞닿고 싶어 했던 세계 미술계의 보편가치가 바로 우리 안에 내재함을 목격하고자 했다. 구동희, 김두진, 김상돈, 노재운, 그리고 금혜원, 노충현, 정재호 등의 작품들을 만나볼 것인데, 1990년대를 통해서 얻은 '동시대적', '동시대성'이란 단순 특정 시기 구분을 지칭하는 표현이 아니라, 일종의 관점, 태도 혹은 패러다임과 관계된 것임을 이해하고자 했다.

불일치의 활성화

앞서 언급했던 정보통신과학기술의 발달이라든지 대중소비문화의 확산 등은 당시 젊은 세대들을 자극했고, 당대 세대들은 스스로의 시각과 태도를 공중에 드러내고 나누기를 전개했는데, 이에 문화예술 기획에 있어 수용의 문제는 주요 변수로 작동하였다. 1990년대에서 2000년대로 이어지면서 이전과 비할 바 없이 확장된 영향력을 가진 대중소비문화의 가소적 양상은 과거 모던 담론에서 외면받았던 욕망, 감정, 몸 등을 새삼 관심 이슈로 다루었다. 지속적으로 유동하고 확장하는 사회적 상황과 도시환경 내에서, 그리고 그것을 통해 직조된 문화토양 속에서 성장한 세대들에게 있어 그들의 작업과 활동은 원천적으로 복합적이고 다중적 양상을 띨 수밖에 없었다.[2]

1990년대 초 한국 미술계 내 소위 '포스트모더니즘 논쟁' 뿐 아니라 우리 현대미술에 영향을 미치는 다양한 담론과 비평적 논의가 전개되었다. 1990년대를 뚫고 성장한 작가들은 집단주의, 진영 논리, 진영 간의 헤게모니 다툼과는 차원 다른 노력과 실천을 통해 미술적 성취를 이루고자 했다. 그래서 신세대 감각을 통해 발현한 미술이라든지 퍼포먼스, 대형 설치미술, 여성주의 미술, 한국적 개념주의 미술, 그리고 새로이 주목받은 매체인 미디어 작업 등이 작가들의 작업에서 다채롭게 드러났다.

2   이영미, 「총론」, 한국예술종합학교
    한국예술연구소 엮음,
    『한국현대예술사대계 VI-1990년대』
    (서울: 시공사, 2005), 22, 27.

'동시대성'을 단순한 시간적 차원의 개념이 아니라 기존의 헤게모니 구조에 대한 문제 제기와 관련하여 다루어 볼 때, 이를 잘 설명할 수 있는 매체가 바로 미디어 작업이라 하겠다. 우리 싱글채널 비디오의 본격적인 개화 시기를 1990년대 말에서 2000년대 초로 볼 수 있는 연유는 대중, 영상, 문화의 시대 맥락과 맞닿아 있다. 그리고 비선형적 이야기 구조, 분절적 화면 전개, 시간적 굴절, 시청각적 감각의 뒤틀림 등 지금과 같은 미디어 영상 시대에는 더 이상 낯설지 않으나 이 어법들이 작품에 본격적으로 드러나기 시작한 때는 1990년대 후반이라 할 수 있다. 이번 전시에서 김세진, 박화영, 유비호, 함양아 등 이들 작가 초기 미디어 작업과 김아영, 남화연, 안정주 등의 2010년대 미디어 작업, 그러니까 이질적이고 복합적인 시공간의 관계망과 관련한 동시대 작가의 작품을 통해 한국 동시대 미술의 흐름을 보다 깊숙이 들여다보고자 했다.

미래 간섭 혹은 미래 개입

우리 사회는 서구가 그랬듯이 모던 이후 탈모던, 자본주의 이후 후기자본주의 등의 순차적으로 옮아가는 경로나 시공간적 상황과는 전혀 다르게, 지금도 끝나지 않은 전근대, 근대, 그리고 근대 이후가 중첩되고 응축된 상황 속에서 흔치 않게 여러 상황과 조건들이 뒤섞이고 거듭 고쳐지고 겹쳐진 '현장'으로 자리하고 있다. 이러한 점에서 한국 현대미술의 동시대성은 이번 전시 작가들의 작품을 통해서 볼 수 있는 바, 우리의 특수한 시공간 내 혼종과 굴절의 상황적 짜임을 통해서 확보된 것이라 하겠다. 흥미로운 점은 우리 미술이 그렇게 맞닿고 싶어 했던 세계 동시대 미술의 보편 가치가 바로 우리 안에 자리하고 있음을 역설적으로 드러내는 것이다.

한국 동시대 미술 연구에 있어 미술관이 동시대성의 맥락이 형성된 시기 작가들의 작품을 비롯하여 그와 이어진 차원의 작품들을 수집, 소장하고 있다는 점을 주목할 이유는 분명하다. 대내외적 사회 환경뿐 아니라, 미술계 내부적으로도 다양한 변화를 맞이했던 시기였고, 또한 소위 한국적 모더니즘 미술과 민중미술의 논쟁적 구도가 지나간 자리에 발생한 미술은 그 시기뿐 아니라 지금의 미술을 읽어내는 데에도 중요한 의미를 가진다. 서두에도 밝힌 바, 1990년대에서 2000년대로 이어지는 시기의 미술에 대한 밀도 있는 연구를 위해서는 더욱 지속적이고 충분한 연구와 수집이 필요하다. 움직이고 있는 동시대 미술의 줄기를 단숨에 정돈하는 것은 적절하지 않을 뿐더러 가능하지도 않다. 다만 지금 동시대성을 이해하기 위해 그 형성 맥락의 촉발 지대를 알아내는 것은 중요한 과제이다. 우리 동시대 미술의 토양으로 혼종적이고 이질적 환경과 상황을 풀이하는 데 적합한 인식적 태도를 발견하려는 노력은 주저할 이유가 없다.

Back to the Future: An Exploration of Contemporaneity in Korean Contemporary Art

Kim Hyoungmi
Curator, National Museum of Modern and Contemporary Art, Korea

Back to the Future: An Exploration of Contemporaneity of Korean Contemporary Art is an exhibition organized with the intention of sharing artwork from the collection of the National Museum of Modern and Contemporary Art, Korea (MMCA) with the public. Covering artworks acquired by the museum over a five-year period, from 2018 to 2022, the exhibition thoroughly examines the characteristics of noteworthy acquisitions from this time. In accordance with MMCA acquisition policies and directions, the artwork acquired each year has shown an even distribution in terms of era, genre, and theme with pieces acquired over the recent five-years being no exception. One of the most important characteristics observed in these particular acquisitions is that a large number of works are from the artists who demonstrate the contemporaneity of Korean contemporary art, based on the transitional historical period of the 1990s, including figures such as Kong Sunghun, Kim Beom, and Bahc Yiso.

While the chronological emphasis may be on the 1990s, the exhibition includes works ranging from the late 1980s to 2010 in its scope of influence; in doing so, it hopes to highlight the time in which many of the featured artists were establishing their artistic identity—between the late 1980s and early 1990s— along with some of their more recent artistic activities. Also presented among the museum's acquisitions are works by artists who grew up amid a climate, in the late 20th and early 21st centuries, that saw the intersection and coexistence of analog and digital. Later emerging in the scene, they have since established themselves as important presences in the Korean contemporary art world. Furthermore, the exhibition seeks to provide viewers with the opportunity to observe works by artists who, back then, contributed notably to the creation of the context behind the contemporaneity of Korean contemporary art; this is evident in works created by currently practicing artists in the present day. Major artworks from this period are still being added to the museum's collection, and while it is impossible to show all previously acquired works here, the exhibition, through the selected artists and artworks, offers a chance to reexamine Korean art during a period that, while belonging to the not-too-distant past, still warrants being historicized.

Back to the Future

The exhibition shares its title *Back to the Future* with a Hollywood film released in 1985 (1987 in Korea). The protagonist Marty uses a time machine to travel back 30 years in time from 1985. In his journeys between the past, present, and future, he ends up entangled in a complex situation. Despite its more or less linear presentation, the film's story deals with clashing times and places. The year of *Back to the Future*'s Korean release in 1987 fell during a period that is often referred to as the starting point for the emergence of "contemporaneity" in Korean contemporary art. Popular culture—especially music, movies, and comics—had an enormous impact on Korean young generation during the late 1980s and 1990s alongside the rapid political, social, and economic transformations occurring in and outside Korea at the time. The progressive generational shift that unfolded with these historical changes may be viewed as the most pivotal transformation of the period. A major mechanism defining the era is the emergence of a generation that unhesitatingly navigated phenomena and circumstances unmarked by previous practices, that which could not be interpreted according to past logic. By following that same complex path, perhaps we can better understand that which is evoked in the present. After all, the "future" seen in *Back to the Future* is our "today."

A New Era of Diversion, and Paradigm Shift in Art

To briefly overview the significant events that occurred in and outside of Korea between the 1980s and 2000s, Korea underwent the June Struggle in 1987, hosted the Asian Games in 1986 and the Summer Olympics in 1998, after which a civil government took office in 1993 to lead to the maturation of democracy, if only on a procedural level. This served as a footing for the operation of social mechanisms distinguished from those of the previous era, such as economic growth and globalization strategies, to assert a real impact on civilian life. Globally, the same period was a historically unprecedented one of great transition. The Berlin Wall fell in 1989, the Eastern European socialist system collapsed to undergo reform, and the dissolution of the Soviet Union in 1991 brought an end to the Cold War era. With that, politics gave way to capital and economic logic, which would gain control of the world order. It was around this time and in the wake of a extreme yet compressed growth that Korea was hit with the Asian Financial Crisis of 1997. The process of recovery that followed made Korean people aware of their power as the foundation and protective force of their country. As such, by the time the era of globalism had dawned towards the end of the 1990s, the quality of universality was shared by the world and understood as something hard-earned through a long social struggle and sacrifice. What's more, the shock of the series of major events that marked the 1990s, along with social changes and economic expansion, would remain imprinted in the minds of the young people living through the period.[1]

Certain aspects of this period are key to understanding the cultural and artistic trends that would ensue—innovation in information and communications technologies and the spread of popular and consumer culture. The advent of the internet accelerated innovation in information and communications science and technologies, enabling real-time connection on a global level. Accordingly, a current of change swept across the Korean art scene between the 1990s and 2000s, the central force of which was the rising generation of

1. Jung Hunyee, "Art," *History of Korean Modern and Contemporary Art VI: 1990s*, a compilation by the Korean National Research Center for the Arts at the Korean National University of Arts (Seoul: Sigongsa, 2005), 269–270.

youth at the time. Characterized by fluidity, or the rejection of stagnation, late-nineties youth culture was quickly transmitted across the country, aided by the rapid commercialization of the internet and a generation that would not hesitate to exploit it.

Recently, so-called "1990s style" has enjoyed popularity with a revival in popular culture. A period of intense historical transformation, this style recalls associations with the social/cultural environment and the different forms of practice that were observed and established at the time. Art from the 1990s and 2000s reflected the monumental changes in the global constitution as well as related developments in Korea's social environment. Contemporary Korean art from this period was both universal and specific and is only properly understood by taking the global dimension and internal contexts unique to Korea into account. "Contemporaneity" enables a deviation from the system that addresses or perceives situations and states in terms of sequential and linear flows of time and space; it relates to valuation that reflect times, places, situations, and conditions that are complex and entangled. By considering the artistic practices of the time, the exhibition attempts to identify which contexts made such perspectives possible. It begins by exhibiting the artworks of Kong Sunghun, Kim Beom, Bahc Yiso, Lee Dongi, Lee Yongbaek, Choi Jeonghwa, and Seo Hyunsuk, collected between 2018 and 2022, as a lens to better understand the establishment of "contemporaneity" in Korean contemporary art.

Heterogeneity and Its Critical Time and Space

Between the late 1980s and early 1990s, Korea faced drastic social changes both domestically and internationally. This had the effect of fostering a robust climate for Korean contemporary art to take on aspects of contemporaneity. Korean society of the 1990s was marked by intersections and clashes between the benefits and drawbacks of the accelerated growth achieved through the rapid industrialization and modernization of the last few decades. Entering the postmodern era, while still facing issues that could not be resolved during the premodern and modern eras, Korea faced an environment in which different time frames were intermingled. Additionally, it was obliged to accept an untrammeled influx of globalization and neoliberalism. Within this dynamic context of chaos and novelty, the geopolitical and historical realities that Korean society faced became, if anything, more clearly defined. Among the artists encountered in this exhibition are some who grew up in and developed their creative capabilities during this period. These figures, whom we might refer to as "wholly contemporary" artists, were not confined by the conventional distinctions of genre or domain. They were quick to observe local and global trends of transformation, adept at strategically using newly developing economic and societal conditions and circumstances, and unhesitant about accepting their environment in terms of popular culture and society. In these ways, they willingly navigated a complex web of real-world relationships.

The internal changes witnessed within the Korean art scene were another remarkable phenomenon of this period. On a surface level, changes included the establishment of numerous major art institutions, such as national and public museums and alternative spaces; the hosting of multiple international art events; the diversification of the art market; and the emergence of art-related magazines and other online or offline media. This meant that Korean contemporary art, in terms of its industry and infrastructure, had caught up to the pace of that of the world.

For a long time now, the Korean art scene has eagerly sought for recognition and inclusion from the global art world. Korean and other non-Western art spheres have striven to stay in touch by participating in international-scale art events such as biennales. To a degree this helped relieve the obsessive desire for acceptance, but whether they can fundamentally homogenize into the global art world still remains a question. Hence, the linear understanding and assessment of their participation in international-scale art events as certificates for contemporaneity would mean failure to read into the heterogeneous and complex network surrounding the concept of "contemporaneity" and the countless and multilayered discussions derived therefrom.

Beyond superficial aspects such as similar formative vocabularies or the sharing of universal qualities with the global art world in the midst of globalism, their artistic practices can be seen as individual expressions rooted in the native soil of a rapidly transforming historical situation, and the resulting diverse hybridity. Through the work of artists who sincerely demonstrated their individual identities within the Korean contemporary art context of the 1990s and early 2000s—and who continue to show their artistic capabilities even today—the exhibition bears witness to how the universal values of global art, that Korean art has long sought to connect with, are already immanent within us. In encountering pieces by the likes of Koo Donghee, Kim Dujin, Kim Sangdon, Rho Jaeoon, Keum Hyewon, Roh Choonghyun, and Jung Jaeho, the exhibition attempts to understand how "the contemporary" and "contemporaneity" of the 1990s do not simply refer to a particular historical division, but rather to something closer to a perspective, attitude, or paradigm.

Energizing Nonconformity

The aforementioned advancements in information and communications technology and spread of popular and consumption cultures provoked the desires intrinsic in the youth at the time, who would openly share their individual views and attitudes with the public. Consequently, the issue of reception itself came to be a key variable in the planning of cultural and artistic projects. Throughout the 1990s and well into the 2000s, the plasticity of popular and consumption cultures, which had grown more influential than ever, manifested in the revisitation of artistic themes previously eschewed by modern discourses such as desire, emotions, and the body. The works and activities of a generation that grew up deeply rooted within cultures bred from ever-fluid social circumstances and a ceaselessly expanding urban environment, were inherently and inevitably complex and heterogeneous in nature.[2]

The Korean art scene in the early 1990s saw the progress of diverse discourses and critical discussions (including the so-called "postmodernism debate") that would go on to influence contemporary artworks to follow. Artists who burgeoned through the 1990s sought to make artistic achievements through honest work and practice rather than through collectivism, that is, by taking political sides or engaging in fights for hegemonic dominance. The artworks produced by this "new generation" of artists would, thus, reveal kaleidoscopic sensibilities, manifesting in various art forms including performance, large-scale installation, feminist art, Korean-style conceptual art, and—in particular—media art, which would go on to gain renewed attention.

If "contemporaneity" is approached as something more than a mere temporal concept, as a matter connected with the problematization of existing hegemonic structures, a particularly good example illustrating this can be found in media-based artwork. The period between the late 1990s and early 2000s is often viewed as true blooming of Korean single-channel video works, because of the relations it bears to the historical context in terms of popular environment, video, and culture. In an age of media and video such as today, approaches such as non-linear narrative structure, segmented screens, temporal refraction, and skewing of visual and auditory sensations no longer seem strange. The late 1990s is perhaps the period in which this sort of vocabulary first became prevalent in artwork. Exploring the early media-based work of artists such as Kim Sejin, Park Hwayoung, Ryu Biho, and Ham Yangah as well as the 2010s-era media artwork of figures like Kim Ayoung, Nam Hwayeon , and An Jungju, the exhibition joins the viewer in observing the currents in Korean contemporary art, through the creations of contemporary artists who relate to disparate and complex temporal and spatial networks.

"Interfering with" or "Intervening in" the Future

Korean society has followed a very different trajectory from the pathways and temporal/spatial circumstances of the West, which moved linearly from the modern to the postmodern era and later from capitalism to late capitalism. From a context in which the premodern, modern, and (currently ongoing) postmodern overlap and condense, we see an unusual case of various situations and conditions existing as an "environment"—intermingled, constantly revised, and overlapping. In that sense, the works of the artists in this exhibition

2. Lee Youngmi, "Introduction," *History of Korean Modern and Contemporary Art VI: 1990s*, a compilation by the Korean National Research Center for the Arts at the Korean National University of Arts (Seoul: Sigongsa, 2005), 22, 27.

offer a glimpse at how the contemporaneity of Korean contemporary art was established through the situational structure of hybridity and refracting from within Korea's specific spatial and temporal context. Ironically, the universal values of global contemporary that many artists pursued were in fact present within our autochthonic time and space.

There is a clear reason, then, for MMCA's focus on acquiring contemporary Korean artworks that were produced by artists working in an era during which the context behind contemporaneity was established, as well as other subsequently created artworks. This period of diverse change occurred not just in the domestic and international social environment, but in the Korean art world itself. Furthermore, the art that emerged in the wake of the polemical context of so-called "Korean modernist art" and Minjung Art (Korean protest art movement of the 1970s and 1980s), holds important significance in interpreting not only that era's art but also today's. As previously mentioned, ample and ongoing collection efforts are needed to aid the in-depth research of art from made during the 1990s and 2000s. Contemporary art is a moving thing, and it is not appropriate to tie it down. However, in order to understand today's contemporaneity, it is important to investigate the origins of its context. There is no cause for hesitation when attempting to discover the most appropriate stance from which to interpret the hybrid and heterogeneous conditions, the matrix, that nurtured Korean contemporary art.

여전히 동시대적인, 1990-2010년대 한국미술

이은주

독립기획자, 미술사가

출현: 집단성에서 개인적 특이성으로

1990년대 말부터 2000년대 초에 대안공간 공모를 통해 첫 개인전을 열었던 신진작가들도 어느덧 한국 미술계의 중견이 되었다. "지금의 동시대성을 이해하기 위한 맥락의 촉발 지점을 알아내는 것"[1]을 시도하는 국립현대미술관의 소장품 특별전 《백 투 더 퓨처: 한국 현대미술의 동시대성 탐험기》의 주축이 되는 것도 이 작가들이다. 실상 현재의 미술계는 'MZ세대'로 일컬어지는 20–30대 작가들이 전 세대와는 결이 다른 문화적 층위를 형성하고 있고, 디지털 기술의 급속한 발전 속에서 무시할 수 없는 양으로 출현하는 신경향들이 얽혀 복잡한 지형도를 이루고 있다. 동시대성이 결국 공동의(con) 시간대(temporary)가 만들어내는 성격을 의미하는 것이자, 오늘날의 세계를 이루는 공동 조건 혹은 총체적인 현재를 상정하며, 더 나아가 가장 현재적인 것을 포함한다고 했을 때, 세대 문화의 큰 전환기인 현시점에서 동시대 미술을 단선적으로 규정하거나 그 발생 지점을 명확하게 지시하는 것은 불가능한 일이다. 그러나 오늘날 제도권 미술계의 주요한 시각 언어가 이전 세대의 것과 이질적인 맥락을 형성하며 첫 출현한 시기를 특정할 수는 있을 것이다.

1980년대의 주요 기관에서 열렸던 전시 제목을 살펴보면 《사실과 현실 80 회화전》(미술회관, 1980), 《현실과 발언》(동산방 화랑, 1980), 《오늘의 전통회화 '81》(관훈미술관, 1981), 《현대 종이의 조형-한국과 일본전》(국립현대미술관, 1982), 《물(物)의 체험전》(전화랑, 후화랑, 1985), 《한국화 100년전》(호암갤러리, 1986) 등 '사실', '현실', '전통', '물질'이라는 개념들이 저변에 있음을 확인할 수 있다.[2] 이와 같은 전시 제목은 당대 미술 담론의 거점이 현실 참여를 강조했던 민중미술 계열, 물질을 통한 탈속적 수행을 추구했던 단색화 계열, 전통을 현대화하려는 한국화 그룹, 일부는 1970년대 말 민전을 통해 부상한 극사실주의 계열에 있었음을 드러낸다.

그런데 '현실', '물질' 등의 중심 주제를 보여주는 1980년대 전시 제목 가운데 간간이 눈에 들어오는 것은 '청년' 혹은 '신세대', '신진'이라는 단어들이다. 《한국미술 20대의 '힘' 전》(아람문화회관, 1985)이 급진적 신세대 민중미술을 표방하긴 했지만, 연례 전시인 《청년 작가》(국립현대미술관, 1981–),[3] 《물(物)의 신세대 전》(관훈미술관, 1986)이나 《'87 신진 청년작가들에 의한 한국 현대미술 최전선 전》(관훈미술관, 1987), 《30대 전》(미술회관, 1988), 『계간미술』의 기획으로 서성록, 성완경, 오광수 등 평론가 11명이 작가를 선정한 《한국 현대미술 신세대 16인》(신세계미술관, 1988) 등에서는 새로운 경향의 신예 작가가 소개되었다.[4]

1. 국립현대미술관 김형미 학예연구사의 《백 투 더 퓨처: 한국 현대미술의 동시대성 탐험기》 기획안을 참조함.

2. 김달진미술연구소(편), 『한국미술 전시자료집 III: 1980–1989』(서울: 예술경영지원센터, 김달진미술연구소, 2017) 참고.

3. 1981년 《청년 작가》로 시작된 국립현대미술관의 연례 전시는 1990년 제6회 전시부터 《젊은 모색》으로 명칭이 변경되었다.

4. 주 2 참조.

이러한 전시에는 고낙범, 노상균, 오상길, 육근병, 이불, 조덕현, 최정화 등 '타라',
'메타복스', '로고스&파토스', '뮤지엄', '레알리떼 서울'과 같이 1980년대 소그룹에
속한 작가들이 참여했는데, 이들은 현실과 물질에 대한 태도를 새롭게 설정하면서
개인성을 강조하고 거대담론에서 벗어났다.[5] 창립전에서 난지도는 정치사회적
현실 대신 "현실 생활"[6]을 얘기했고, 메타복스는 "익명화된 물성의 극복"[7]을,
로고스&파토스는 "개개인의 활동적이고 열의에 찬 독창력 발휘"[8]를, 뮤지엄은
"지극히 사적인 관심에서 출발한 개인적인 설화"[9]를 강조했다. 이들은 개인화된
시각으로 바라본 현실과 물질이라는 주제를 생활, 오브제, 몸, 정체성과 같은 새로운
화두와 연결시키며 1990년대 한국미술의 주체로 부상했다. 한편으로 해외 유학길에
오른 '386 세대' 작가들도 당대 해외 미술의 영향으로 민중미술과 단색화와는 다른
어법을 구축하며 한국 미술계에 등장했다.

　　　　개인적 특이성을 강조하는 미술로의 변화는 1990년대 후반 미술계에 출현한
이른바 'X세대'에 의해서 가속화된다. 이들은 민주화운동을 현장보다 선배들의
구술이나 미디어를 통해 접한 세대이다. 1987년 6.29 선언 이후 민주화의 점진적
실현으로, 독재 타도를 외치던 대학가의 구호는 학내 민주화나 학생 복지 이슈로
변화되었다. 1988년 서울 압구정동에 맥도날드 1호점이 개점하면서 서울판
'로데오 거리'를 중심으로 소비문화의 주체인 일명 '오렌지 족'이 출현했고,
독재정권에 대한 저항적 청년문화를 대변하던 로큰롤과 포크는 1992년 「특종! TV
연예」 프로그램을 통해 공중파에 데뷔한 서태지와 아이들의 「난 알아요」(1992)로
교체되었다. 할리우드 영화, J-팝과 애니메이션을 즐기며 성장한 X세대가 저항의
대상으로 삼았던 것은 정권이 아니라 서태지와 아이들의 「교실 이데아」(1994)에서
상정된 바와 같은 권위주의와 획일화된 집단성이었다. 이들의 청년문화는 광장
중심의 투쟁적 집회 문화에서 대중적 소비 공간에 개인들이 이합집산하는 문화로
이행했다.

이처럼 X세대 미술가들은 민중미술과 단색화 중심의 담론에 균열을 일으킨 소그룹
작가들이나 민전 출신의 극사실주의 작가들과도 완전히 다른 문화적 기반에서
출발했다. 이들은 자신들의 일상적 경험으로부터 나오는 개인적 특이성을
미술 언어의 기반으로 삼았다. 그것이 어디에도 소속되지 못한 관찰자로서의
시선이든, 집단적 발화가 사라진 공백에 남은 허무함과 불안이든, 욕망을 추동하는
소비문화의 주체이든 일상적 소회이든 간에, 특이점이 있는 개성적 언어와
스타일을 만드는 것이 곧 작가적 태도의 선결 조건이 되었다. 이들이 견인했던

5. 1981년 5월 'TA-RA(Tabula Rasa)',
　1985년 2월 '난지도', 1985년
　9월 'META-VOX', 1986년 8월
　'로고스&파토스', 1987년 1월 '레알리떼
　서울', 2월 'MUSEUM'의 창립전이
　열렸다.

6. 난지도, 「우리의 입장」, 제1회 난지도
　전시 리플릿(서울: 관훈미술관, 1985);
　주 2 참조(55 재수록).

7. 이일, 「창립전 서문」, 제1회 META-VOX
　전시 리플릿(서울: 후화랑, 1985); 주 2
　참조(57 재수록).

8. 로고스&파토스, 서문, 제1회
　로고스&파토스 전시 리플릿(서울:
　관훈미술관, 1986); 주 2 참조(67 재수록).

9. 윤진섭, 「당돌한 표현력의 결집」, 제1회
　MUSEUM 전시 리플릿(서울: 관훈미술관,
　1987); 주 2 참조(75 재수록).

2000년대 미술은 집단 미학의 구심점 없이 시대 현상에 반응한 개인화된 언어들이 이합집산하며 얽혀있는, 다원화된 증후라고 할 수 있다.

이처럼 개인주의에 기반한 X세대의 사적이고 산발적인 언어를 미술제도 속에 수렴하여 사회적 의미를 부여한 것은 1990년대 중반 이후 동시다발적으로 출현한 신세대 플랫폼들이다. 1996년 최정화가 설치미술로 인테리어를 하여 개장한 명륜동의 '살바'는 어어부밴드, 삐삐밴드가 공연하는 등 예술과 유흥이 섞이는 언더그라운드 문화의 거점이었고, 작가들의 전시 뒤풀이 장소였다.[10] 1998년 서울에 개관한 아트선재센터는 해외 미술의 트렌드를 소개했고, 아트선재센터와 사무소(SAMUSO)를 기반으로 한 김선정의 큐레이팅은 2000년대 이후 한국 작가들의 활동을 국제 미술의 흐름과 연동하는 역할을 했다.[11]

무엇보다 대안공간의 역할이 컸다. 1998년 쌈지 창작 스튜디오가, 1999년에는 대안공간 풀, 대안공간 루프, 프로젝트 스페이스 사루비아다방, 2000년에는 쌈지 스페이스와 인사미술공간이 개관했다. 이어서 2세대 대안공간이 문을 열었는데, 2002년에는 보충대리공간 스톤앤워터, 대안공간 반디, 2003년에는 아트스페이스 휴, 브레인 팩토리가 개관했으며, 2004년 대안공간 팀프리뷰, 2006년에는 오픈스페이스 배가 개관했다. 그 외에도 갤러리 꽃, 갤러리 숲, 대안공간 미끌, 갤러리 킹 등 수많은 후속 대안공간이 연이어 생겼다. 2005년에는 인사미술공간을 주축으로 비영리전시공간협의회(대안공간 네트워크)가 출범하여 공적 재원을 토대로 청년작가를 지원하는 비영리 전시공간의 체제가 확립되었다. 미술대전 대신 대안공간을 통해 데뷔하는 시대로의 전환이 이루어진 것이다. 2006년에는 비영리전시공간협의회가 박찬경을 프로젝트 디렉터로 한 'AFI(Artist Forum International)'를 조직하고 《공공의 순간(Public Moment)》이라는 국제 전시와 공공성에 관한 프로젝트, 작가 지원 방향을 모색하는 워크숍을 대대적으로 기획하며 결집력을 대외적으로 보여주기도 했다.[12] 이러한 상황은 대안공간이 단순히 대안적인 역할을 도모하는 것을 넘어 영향력 있는 미술제도권으로 자리 잡게 되었음을 보여준다.

10. 황동일, 「종합문화공간 살바: 우리 것… 남의 것… 키치 & 고급 다 있어요」, 『한국일보』, 1997년 4월 14일 자, 21면 참고. 살바 이전에도 놀이문화와 예술이 결합된 장소로 스페이스 오존(1989년 개관), 발전소(1992년 개장), 곰팡이(1994년 개장) 등 상업공간과 연합된 예술공간들이 형성되어 있었다. 문혜진, 『90년대 한국 미술과 포스트모더니즘: 동시대 미술의 기원을 찾아서』(서울: 현실문화연구, 2015), 286 참고.

11. 이러한 성과는 2009-2010년 LACMA(Los Angeles County Museum of Art)와 휴스턴 미술관(The Museum of Fine Arts, Houston)에서 김선정, 린 젤레반스키(Lynn Zelevansky), 크리스틴 스타크맨(Christine Starkman)의 공동기획으로 열린 《Your Bright Future: 12 Contemporary Artists from Korea》전으로 이어졌다. 이 전시에는 구정아, 김범, 김수자, 김홍석, 박이소, 박주연, 서도호, 양혜규, 임민욱, 장영혜 중공업, 전준호, 최정화가 참여했다.

12. 이처럼 비영리전시공간협의회가 대외적으로 결집력을 보여준 해인 2006년 발행한 『도어투도어 4』 자료집에 따르면, 쌈지 스페이스, 대안공간 풀, 대안공간 루프, 프로젝트 스페이스 사루비아 다방, 인사미술공간, 갤러리 정미소, 보충대리공간 스톤앤워터, 브레인 팩토리, 대안공간 반디, 스페이스 빔, 아트스페이스 휴, 오픈스페이스 배가 비영리전시공간협의회 회원으로 등록되어 있다. (사)비영리전시공간협의회(편), 『도어투도어 4』(서울: (사)비영리전시공간 협의회, 2006), 97-99 참고.

한편으로 2000년대 이후에는 아카데믹한 미술대학의 커리큘럼이 수용하지 못하는 현장성을 보완하기 위한 대안적 프로그램의 일환으로 다양한 신진작가 프로그램이 기획되었는데, 대표적 사례로 2000년대 초반 비영리전시공간협의회에서 기획한 지방 순회 크리틱 프로그램 '도어투도어(Door to Door)', 2005년 인사미술공간의 신진작가 성장 프로그램 '신진작가수첩'이 있었다. '신진작가수첩'의 일환으로 기획된 《열전》을 통해 데뷔한 신진작가군이 형성되기도 했다. 또한 2000년 에르메스 재단 미술상, 2001년 송은미술대상, 2001년 삼성미술관(당시 호암미술관)의 《아트스펙트럼》전, 2004년 《금호 영아티스트》전과 같은 사립미술관 수상 제도 혹은 공모전으로 신진미술가의 활동 무대가 대폭 늘어났다. 이처럼 신진작가의 빠른 미술계 데뷔가 보편화된 가운데 미술시장 진출도 빨라졌는데, 2005년 이후에는 권오상, 이동욱, 정수진 등 대안공간 전시로 주목받은 신진작가들이 아라리오갤러리와 파격적인 전속계약을 맺으며 화제가 되었다. 이처럼 신진작가 지원 체제가 제도화되면서 작가들의 개별화된 언어는 다양성과 실험성이라는 큰 스펙트럼 안에 수렴되었고, 특정한 미술 경향보다 전시공간을 중심으로 작가들의 군집이 형성되는 뚜렷한 변화가 나타났다.

예술-상업-비영리-공공 영역 사이에 다양한 거점들이 형성되는 이러한 변화 속에서 미술과 현실 사회의 관계도 다양화되었다. 1994년 국립현대미술관에서 열린 《민중미술 15년: 1980–1994》전을 통해 민중미술이 역사의 한 장으로 편입된 이후, 민중미술 계보를 잇는 신세대 미술, 이른바 포스트민중미술 진영은 대안공간 풀의 전시, 미술저널 『포럼A』(1998–2005)의 간행, 인사미술공간이 발행한 『볼(BOL)』(2005–2008)의 편집과 집필을 통해 제도비판 담론을 이어갔다. 그러나 유희와 희화화를 전략으로 삼은 조습의 작업이나 자본주의 도시 생태의 문제를 제기하면서도 한편으로 에르메스 매장의 윈도 디스플레이를 담당한 플라잉시티의 전방위적 활약에서 드러나듯이, 포스트 민중미술 작가의 활동은 종종 대중문화나 자본주의 상품 세계와 연합되기도 했다. 대표적 포스트 민중미술 작가이자 대안공간 풀의 운영진이었던 박찬경은 2004년 에르메스 재단 미술상을 수상하면서 과거 민중미술 작가와는 다른 패셔너블한 도시 엘리트의 인상을 남겼는데, 이는 '아방가르드'와 '프랙티스'의 의미가 민주화 항쟁 시기와는 다른 '트렌드'와 '지식의 최전선'으로 변화되었음을 보여주는 흥미로운 시각적 표상이었다.

양상: 미술에서 시각문화로

1990년대의 주요 기획 전시 제목을 살펴보면 1980년대와 확연히 달라진 미술계의 지형을 읽을 수 있다. 《문화와 삶의 해석》(금호미술관, 1990), 《썬데이 서울》(소나무갤러리, 1990), 《도시 대중 문화》(덕원미술관, 1992), 《여성,

그 다듬과 힘»(한국미술관, 1994), «인간과 기계: 테크놀로지 아트»(동아갤러리, 1995), «도시와 영상»(서울시립미술관, 1996), «아파트먼트: 사물과의 우연하고 행복한 만남»(갤러리아트빔, 1997), «현실과 환상: 사진의 시각적 확장»(국립현대미술관, 1998), «코리안 팝»(성곡미술관, 1999)[13]과 같은 제목들에서 사회 현실에 대한 참여의식이나 단색화의 탈속적 도인과 같은 태도, 민족주의 대신 도시의 일상과 대중문화가 주요 주제로 부상했음을 알 수 있다. 아울러 비민중미술 계열까지 확장된 여성주의를 가늠할 수 있다. 이러한 전시들은 미술보다 '시각문화'라는 용어에 더 적합한 주제와 형식을 드러냈다. 이처럼 1990년대 이후 전개된 미술의 상황을 이번 전시에 출품된 국립현대미술관 소장품들을 중심으로 살펴보고자 한다.

첫 번째로, 구미의 개념미술과 제도비판 미술의 영향으로 제도에 대한 의심과 성찰이 제기된다. 1990년대 초 김범, 박이소는 집단적 담론으로부터는 거리를 두면서 민중미술과는 다른 시각으로 관습과 제도를 비판하고 성찰하는 태도를 제시했다. 유학 중 미국이나 한국 사회 모두에서 비주류가 됨으로써 생긴 관찰자적 태도가 개념미술의 방법론과 결합되면서, 종래의 한국미술에 없던 새로운 주체로서의 시선을 형성했다고 볼 수 있다.[14] 김범은 관람객으로 하여금 이미지에 대한 통념적 기대와 불일치하는 상황에 직면하게 함으로써 관습에 거리를 두고 관찰자적 사고를 하게 만든다. 그는 미국 TV에서 방영한 유명 요리사의 요리법을 따라 한 <무제(닭 요리하기)>(1991)에서 실제 닭 대신 그려진 이미지를 사용하여 의도적으로 허무한 유머를 발생시켜서 이미지와 실재의 간극에 주목하게 하고 규정된 가치들을 회의하게 하는 지적 성찰을 유도했다.

박이소 역시 미술작품이란 "모든 것에 대한 나의 끝없는 의심을 정당화하는 과정"이라고 밝힌 바 있다.[15] 그는 대한민국의 규범적 남성 주체에 동화될 수 없는 정서적 거리감을 유지하면서, 그들에 의해 숭상되는 것들을 냉소적으로 바라보았다. <2010년 세계에서 가장 높은 건축물 1–10위>(2003)에서는 제목과는 달리 수공적 오브제로 만들어낸 의도적인 허술함과 취약함으로 허탈한 실소를 자아내면서 개발 논리와 성공 신화로 세워진 가치들을 무력화한다.[16] 박이소는 소속될 수도 없고 소속되기도 싫은 사회에 대한 거리감이 야기하는 권태와 무기력감을 동력 삼아, 한국의 압축성장을 이룬 '하면 된다' 식의 새마을운동 슬로건에 대한

13. 김달진미술연구소(편), 『한국미술 전시자료집 IV: 1990–1999』 제1권(서울: 예술경영지원센터, 김달진미술연구소, 2018), 16–118 참고.
14. 이러한 관점과 관련하여, 미술사학자 우정아는 박이소와 안규철을 한국미술의 "개념적 흐름의 시조격"으로 보면서, "이들의 작품에서 마침내 군부독재를 종식시키고 민주화를 이루어 냈던 '386 세대' 혹은 '운동권' 엘리트들이

공유했던 국가와 사회에 대한 부채 의식이 지속적으로 드러나는데도, 미술의 정치적 가능성에 대해 회의적이거나 냉소적이었던 이유는 바로 그 혁명 시기에 이들이 한국의 밖에 있었기 때문이다."라고 진단한 바 있다. 우정아, 「1990년 이후 한국미술의 개념적 전환」, 『한국미술 1900–2020』(서울: 국립현대미술관, 2021), 415.
15. 박이소, 「작품에 대하여」(2000),

국립현대미술관(편), 『박이소: 기록과 기억』(과천: 국립현대미술관, 2018), 1.
16. 박이소는 "벽 위에 고정되어 있는 미술작품은 취약하고 비효율적이다. 그러나 바로 그 때문에 엄청난 속도와 가상공간의 당면 환경에 대해 효과적이거나 힘찬 것은 아닐지라도 상당히 흥미로운 저항의 가능성을 가지고 있다고 본다."라고 언급했다. 같은 책, 1. 참고.

반대급부로서의 취약함을 미학적으로 형식화했다고 할 수 있다.

이와 같은 우회적인 비판의 태도는 2010년대 이후의 작품에도 이어진다. 보다 젊은 세대인 구동희 역시 일상적 맥락을 짓궂게 비틀어 관습적 기대를 배반한다. 예컨대 영상작업 〈타가수분〉(2016)에서 구동희는 욕망의 해소라는 하나의 축 안에 대중적인 호프집과 은밀하고 사적인 고급 욕실이라는 2개의 공간을 배치하고, 마치 개체가 다른 2종끼리 수분하듯 자본주의 체제에서의 경제 계급적 지위와 공간적 기능이 각기 다른 두 장소를 점진적으로 서로 간섭시키며 부조리하게 연결되는 서사 구조를 만들었다. 분명한 의미 전달을 끝까지 유보하는 이 작품은 기묘한 뒷맛을 남기면서 결과적으로 작가 자신이 서사의 출발점에 설정해 두었던 모든 관습적 전제들을 의심하게 만든다. 한편으로 대안공간 풀을 중심으로 활동했던 김상돈은 포스트 민중미술 계보의 사회비판을 조형성이 강한 오브제와 설치미학을 통해 환유적으로 구현했다. 그의 〈모뉴멘트 제로〉(2014)는 국가 이데올로기의 상징인 영웅 기념비 대신 공권력의 오작동에 의해 희생되고 사라진 이들을 위한 기념비를 제작하여 사진으로 촬영한 작업으로, 사회비판적 메시지를 전하되 그것을 김홍석, 정서영 등 1990년대 후반부터 개념미술 기반의 독일 유학파 출신 작가들이 구사했던 바와 같은 오브제 미학 안에 장착하고 있다.

　　　두 번째로, 도시와 일상을 다루는 새로운 태도가 제기된다. 민중미술에서 자본주의의 영역으로 상정되었던 도시는 1990년대 후반부터 작가들의 일상적 삶의 터전으로 미술에 등장했다. 이러한 작업의 모태로서, 이번 전시에는 출품되지 않았으나 최진욱의 작업을 빼놓을 수 없을 것이다. 최진욱은 날 선 시선으로 도시를 바라보면서도, 민중미술계 리얼리즘의 직설적 비판에서 벗어나 극사실주의 회화에서 나타난 일상적 도시 소재와 회화형식 탐구의 계보를 잇는다. 그러면서도 그는 화가의 자의식과 서울의 로컬리티가 함께 투영된 작품들을 통해 민중미술의 서술적 구상도 극사실주의의 회화술도 아닌, 화가의 일상과 회화의 리얼리티가 하나로 수렴되는 지점을 성취했다. 이러한 맥락과 이어지는 더 젊은 세대의 공성훈, 김수영, 노충현, 박주욱, 이문주, 이제, 정재호 등 회화 작가들은 2000년대 이후 자신들의 일상 무대인 도시 풍경을 찍고 사진의 사실성을 회화성으로 전환하는 작업을 했다. 이들에게 있어서 도시는 잠재적 서사를 담고 있는 장소인 동시에 사각의 프레임 안에 안착시켜야 할 조형적 대상이었다. 일상적인 인물들의 사진으로부터 출발하여 회화 자체의 미학을 추구해나간 강석호, 박진아, 서동욱, 이광호 역시 이와 같은 맥락에 있는 작가들이다.

특히 이번 전시에 출품된 공성훈, 노충현, 정재호의 작품들은 회화 고유의 미학적 장치를 통해서 일상적 도시 풍경에 남은 제도적 잔재와 그것에 동화되지 못하는 심리적 상태를 함께 드러낸다. 공성훈은 2000년대 초반 도시 개발로 낙후한 것이 되어버린 벽제 지역 풍경의 어색함과 그 안에 도사리는 욕망의 불길한 증후를 그려냈고, 노충현은 남영동 대공분실처럼 폭력적 제도의 잔재로 남아있는 장소나 한강고수부지처럼 멋없이 개발된 도시 풍경으로부터의 소격감, 그럼에도 불구하고

이미 일상의 터전이 된 이러한 장소에서 매일 체감하게 되는 정서적 온도를
포착했다. 서민 아파트의 파사드를 동양화법으로 구현함으로써 주목받은 정재호는
도시 개발의 유토피아적 청사진과 낙후된 현실 간의 격차를 주지시키며 그 사이를
서민적 삶의 질감으로 채웠다.

    도시를 바라보는 이러한 관점은 사진이나 영상매체에서도 발견된다. 2000년대
이후에는 독일 유형학적 사진의 영향으로 금혜원, 최원준 등 서울 도시 시스템에
대한 기호가 될 수 있는 장소들을 연작으로 촬영하는 사진작가가 출현했다.
금혜원은 2000년대 중반 재개발 공사 현장에 파란색 방수포들이 뒤덮여 있는
풍경을 사진으로 기록한 〈푸른 영토〉(2007–2010) 연작을 발표했다. 그는
이 작업에서 동양화과 출신 작가로서 이상적 자연관을 내재한 산수화의 구도를
연상시키는 방식으로 재개발 장소를 포착함으로써, 자연을 인공물로 영토화시킨
기이한 디스토피아적 상황을 전했다. 금혜원의 또 다른 연작 〈도심〉(2010–
2011)에서 무감정한 시선으로 촬영된 도심 속 폐기물처리시설은 폐기물을 끝없이
양산하는 도시의 거대 시스템을 함의하는 것이다.
한편으로 서현석은 영상 작업을 통해 이상적 도시에 대한 건축적 비전과 현실
도시의 간극에 주목했다. 그는 주로 서구 모더니즘의 이상이 투영된 근대화 과정의
도시 건설에 대해 비판적으로 성찰했는데, 그중 〈잃어버린 항해〉(2011–2018)는
박정희 정권 때 추진된 한국 최초의 주상복합 건물인 세운상가를 주제로 한
다큐멘터리 형식의 작품이다. 서현석은 이 작품에서 르 코르뷔지에의 집합주택의
이상적 비전이 독재정권 아래 경제 개발의 이상이라는 전혀 다른 모델 속에
이식되는 과정을 인터뷰와 자료를 통해 객관적으로 밝혀내면서, 실제적 삶과
통합되지 못하는 거대 도시개발계획의 문제점을 인식하게 만들었다.

    세 번째로 드러나는 것은 소비문화와 대중문화에 대한 수용이다. 1992년
《도시·대중·문화》 전을 기획한 백지숙은 전시 서문에서 "대중문화의 생산적
측면에 대한 이해에 기초하여 대중문화 산물의 현상적 특성들을 더 민감하게
읽어내고 그 어법들을 정확하게 꿰는 일"이 현재 필요하다고 언급했다.[17] 자본주의
대중문화의 파급력을 미술이 감당해야 할 시대로 접어들었음을 인식한 것이다.
'가슴시각연구소'의 대표로서 공간 연출가와 같은 태도로 예술과 상업을 혼종한
최정화는 소비사회로 진입하는 시대적 변화를 함의하는 위치를 지닌다. 그의
작업은 1990년대 을지로의 하위문화와 엘리트 미학 간의 낙차를 전략적으로
활용하면서, 저렴한 서민적 생활용품을 예술상품으로 포섭한 측면이 분명 있다.
그러나 한편으로 1980년대 민중미술에서 민정기의 의도적인 키치가 제기한 바 있던

17. 백지숙. 「도시·대중·문화」,
    『도시·대중·문화』전 도록(서울:
    덕원미술관, 1992); 백지숙,
    『본 것을 걸어가듯이: 어느 큐레이터의
    글쓰기』(서울: 미디어버스, 2018), 28
    재수록.

B급 문화의 소통 가능성을 소비사회의 문맥에 최적화하여, 예술의 저변을 확장한 것도 사실이다. 이러한 양가성을 내재한 최정화의 작품은 소비문화가 예술까지 이입되는 시대의 증후를 명확하게 보여준다.[18]

한편으로 이동기는 작가의 주관성 대신 대중적 아이콘과 같은 이미지를 의도적으로 채택하고 변용함으로써 소비문화 속에서 자란 첫 세대로서의 위치를 시각화했다. 그가 1993년 첫 발표한 '아토마우스' 캐릭터는 아톰과 미키마우스를 보고 자란 세대적 정체성을 반영하는 표상이다. 이동기는 스스로 자신의 작품에 오리지널리티가 없으며 "아무 것도 창조하지 않는 작가"가 되고 싶다고 언급했다.[19] 이러한 태도를 보여주는 이동기의 〈남과 여〉(1990)는 실존적 무게를 지우고 소비사회에서 유통되는 가벼운 커뮤니케이션 기호들로서 변환된 남녀의 모습을 구현한 작품이다.

네 번째로 언급할 수 있는 것은 영상매체 형식에 대한 탐구이다. 아날로그에서 디지털로의 전환기였던 1990년대 영상작가들은 전 시대 비디오 아트의 범주를 설치와 결합하거나 기술적으로 진보된 매체특정성을 실험하는 방식으로 확장해 나갔다. 이용백은 한국 미술계에서 영상매체가 익숙하지 않았던 1990년대 초반부터 조소, 설치, 영상 등 매체 간 융합과 컴퓨터를 활용한 영상 기술적 실험을 일찍이 시도했던 작가이다. 특히 그는 영상의 미장센과 관객 경험의 역학을 영리하게 활용했다. 그의 〈기화되는 것들(포스트 아이엠에프)〉(1999–2000)은 IMF 이후의 공황 상태에 대한 발언인 동시에, 퍼포먼스와 영상매체의 결합, 관객이 3차원 공간 설치의 일부로서 영상을 바라봄으로써 야기되는 몰입과 관조 사이의 효과를 작품의 일부로 끌어들인 점에서도 주목된다. 2000년대 초반 유비호는 영상매체가 주는 기계적 차가움을 제도비판적 관점과 효과적으로 연합했다. 그는 〈검은 질주〉(2000)에서 검은 실루엣의 인물들이 무한 질주하면서도 제자리를 벗어나지 못하는 가상적 상황을 영상편집술로 구현했는데, 자본주의 성공 신화의 덫에 걸린 꼭두각시 같은 그들의 획일적 몸짓은 영상 말미에 마치 포획당한 동물 같은 모습의 인간 군집과 연결되면서 묵시적인 메시지를 전한다.[20]

한편으로 김세진은 디지털 영상매체의 시간성에 주목했다. 〈되돌려진 시간〉(1998)에서 시간의 물리적 흐름에 역행하는 서사를 구현하여, 시간예술이자

18. 이러한 맥락과 관련하여, 미술사학자 윤난지는 최정화의 작품이 자본주의를 패러디한 점에서는 팝아트와 지평을 나누지만, 거기에 토착문화의 기표들 즉 '버내큘러(vernacular) 요소들'을 얹음으로써 팝아트와의 변별점 또한 확보했다고 지적했다. 윤난지, 「최정화의 플라스틱 기호학」, 『한국 현대미술의 정체』(서울: 한길사, 2018), 577–578. 또한 미술사학자 신정훈은 최정화의 작품이 "무표정한 팝이라기보다 사연이 담겨 심리적으로 자극하는 키치나 버내큘러에 가까웠다"고 보면서, "한국의 압축적 근대화의 부실성에 대한 알레고리, 도시화와 산업화 시대에 양산된 익명 디자인의 미학적 잠재성에 대한 찬사"로 읽혀진다고 언급했다. 신정훈, 「1990년대 이후 한국미술의 공적인 삶」, 『한국미술 1900–2000』(서울: 국립현대미술관, 2021), 383.

19. 김종호, 류한승, 『한국의 젊은 미술가들: 45명과의 인터뷰』(서울: 다빈치기프트,

2006), 142.

20. 자본주의 시스템에 대한 이러한 비판의식은 미디어에 대한 통찰로 이어졌다. 유비호와 양아치는 2002년 2인전 《퍼블릭 셀(Public Cell)》전에서 빅브라더와 같이 인간을 통제하고 이데올로기를 주입하는 미디어 시스템에 대한 경각심을 일깨우고자 했다.

자유 편집이 가능한 영상매체에 특화된 방식으로 시간성을 탐구했다. 영상에서
여성의 눈물은 중력에 저항하듯 거꾸로 올라가고, 영상 루핑에 의해 영속적으로
이어질 듯 처음부터 다시 시작된다. 찰나의 시간을 길게 늘려 역행시키고 끝없이
반복되는 편집술을 통해 김세진은 기억과도 유사한 비선형적이고 심리적인
시공간을 창조했다. 박화영은 <소리>(1998)에서 떠돌이 개를 세미-다큐멘터리
방식으로 촬영했는데, 절대 고독 속에서 살아가는 개와 작가가 교감하는 가상적
순간이 삽입되면서 상상과 실재가 동등한 리얼리티를 갖는 영상매체 특유의 서사를
완성했다. 또한 함양아의 <픽셔너리>(2002–2003)는 픽션을 창조하는 영화 제작자가
처한 다큐멘터리적 상황을 기조로, 영상매체의 필연적 조건인 허구와 현실의
관계성을 제기한 작품이다. 촬영 현장에서 벌어지는 실제적 상황을 영상 작업의
일부로 끌어들임으로써, 픽션을 만들어낸다는 것이 영상 작가에게 있어 가상이 아닌
실제 대상과의 관계성을 수반하는 실존적 조건의 일부라는 점을 상기시켰다.

    2000년대 이후에는 영상문화에 익숙한 세대의 커뮤니케이션 방식이 미술에
수용되면서 인터넷망을 통해 유통되는 웹아트 등의 뉴미디어가 등장했다. 노재운은
개인화된 시각장치인 모니터 앞에서 관람자 스스로 스크롤하고 클릭하여 볼 수
있는 웹아트를 창안하여 2000년 자신이 만든 '비말라키넷(vimalaki.net)'(2000)을
통해 전시했다. 고전영화 클립들의 포스트프로덕션을 기반으로 한 이 작업에서
서사의 흐름은 온전히 관객이 스스로 클릭하는 순서에 따라 결정되는 것이다.
이러한 작업은 1인 미디어 시대에 맞는 새로운 소통 방식을 제안했다는 의미를
지닌다.[21]

2010년대 이후의 뉴미디어 작업들은 일상화된 디지털 미디어 조건 속에서 현실과
가상 사이에 있는 몸의 위상을 다루거나 비물질적인 데이터가 디지털 세계
안에서 저장공간이라는 물리적 자리를 차지하는 상황을 작업 주제로 끌어들이게
된다. 예컨대 김아영은 현재진행형 뉴미디어를 활용하는 대표 작가로서 최근까지
<다공성 계곡> 연작을 통해 디지털 공간에서의 데이터 이동을 이주와 영토, 권력의
문제와 연결하여 제시한 바 있다. 권력에 대한 그의 문제의식은 거문도를 둘러싼
서구 권력 간의 힘의 긴장을 다룬 초기작 <PH 익스프레스>(2011)에서도 나타나고
있다. 또한 2010년 이후에는 3D 그래픽 프로그램을 이용하여 실사 같은 가상
이미지를 만듦으로써 가상과 현실의 경계를 모호하게 하는 작업들도 출현했는데,
3D 프로그램의 정교한 렌더링을 통해 미켈란젤로의 이상적 도상을 사슴 뼈
이미지로 교묘하게 분열시켜 소멸의 이미지로 만든 김두진의 <모세, 죽어가는 노예,
승리>(2016–2017)를 예로 들 수 있다.

21. 노재운은 음악, 문학, 만화 등을 하는
  사람들과 커뮤니케이션하면서 작업을
  만들게 되었다고 밝혔다.또한 웹사이트
  자체를 작품으로 봐도 되고, 개별적인
작업들을 즐겨도 되며, 관객들이 작품
리스트들을 선택적으로 엮어서 작품을
만들어봐도 된다고 언급했다. 같은 책, 58.

다섯 번째로 발견되는 것은 세계화에 대한 반응이다. 1993년 휘트니비엔날레 서울전이 열리고, 1995년 베니스비엔날레 한국관이 개관하는 등 한국미술이 세계미술의 동시대 흐름과 연동되기 시작했고, 2000년대 이후에는 청년 작가들이 다양한 해외 레지던시 프로그램에 참여하며 해외 체류가 일상화되었다. 세계화에 대한 이들의 반응은 2000년대 이후 문화의 전이에 관한 작업들로 나타났다. 출품작은 아니나 박주연의 <모놀로그 모놀로그(Monologue monologue)>(2006)는 원어민 영어 강사가 말하는 모습에 한국 청년이 영어를 읽는 목소리를 립싱크한 작품으로, 지배문화가 이행하고 전이되는 과정을 함의하고 있다. 이러한 주제의식은 2010년대 이후 작품들에서도 발견된다. 남화연은 2000년대 중반부터 관습적 개념이나 이미지의 배후 맥락을 추적하는 작업을 해왔는데, 그의 <약동하는 춤>(2017)은 몸에 얽힌 사회적 맥락을 탐색한 영상 작업이다. 작품 속 세 여성은 할리우드 영화 「플래시 댄스」 속의 춤을 공식처럼 몸에 내재화하는 연습을 각자 계속한 후 함께 군무를 추는데, 그것이 자유로운 몸짓의 표현인지 집단적 가치를 몸에 새기는 것인지 생각하게 만든다. 이 작품은 전형적 미국 영화 속 여성의 몸짓이 북한에서 '약동하는 춤'이라는 정치적 군무로, 한국의 젊은 여성들에게는 댄스 교본으로 수용되는 상황을 계기로 하여, 몸에 얽힌 이데올로기와 그것이 문화권의 특성에 따라 전이되고 번역되는 과정을 함축한다고 할 수 있다.

한편으로 안정주는 중국 공안의 제식훈련 장면과 구호를 타악기 연주처럼 변주한 <Drill>(2005)을 통해 한 사회의 이데올로기가 관광객에게 단지 스타일이나 음향의 차원으로 전이되는 점을 보여준 바 있다. 그는 바르셀로나의 레지던시에 체류하면서 <영원한 친구와 손에 손잡고>(2016)를 제작했다. 바르셀로나 올림픽 공식 주제가 「영원한 친구」와 서울 올림픽 공식 주제가 「손에 손잡고」를 리믹스하여 중계영상과 함께 편집했는데, 통합된 서사를 파괴하는 방식을 통해서 주제가들이 전하려는 세계화의 거대한 아젠다에 대한 몰입을 지연시키고 부풀려진 이상적 메시지를 무력화하는 거리감을 만들어낸다.

지금까지 이번 전시에 출품된 국립현대미술관의 소장품들을 중심으로 X세대의 출현기인 1990년대 말부터 2000년대의 미술, 그 흐름과 이어지는 2010년대까지의 흐름을 살펴보았다. AI의 일상적 출현을 기대하거나 염려하는 현시점에서 1990년대부터 2000년대는 아주 오래된 과거처럼 보이기도 한다. 그러나 이 시기에 등장한 작가들의 시각 언어는 현재적 현상에 반응하면서 여전히 진화하고 있기에 동시대적이다. 1990년대부터 2000년대는 필자가 미술사학과 대학원생으로서 동시대 미술에 관심을 두기 시작하고, 졸업 후 기획자이자 평론가로 한국미술 현장에서 활동한 시기이기도 하다. 역사에 기록되는 장들이 모두 당대에는 긴장과 열기와 다양한 역학 관계 속에서 출현한 사건들의 얽힘이자 최전선의 현장이었다는 점을 생각하면, 역사에서 누락되는 부분을 메우는 것이 불가능하다는 점에 한계를 느끼기도 한다. 그럼에도 불구하고 산발적인 것으로 보였던 경향들에 형태를 부여함으로써 시각을 확보하는 것이 요청되기에, 과거에 대한 서술을 지속적으로 시도할 수밖에 없다. 전시 제목 《백 투 더 퓨처: 한국 현대미술의 동시대성 탐험기》처럼 과거와 현재의 연속적 맥락을 따라 시간여행 하듯 거슬러 올라가는 이 전시를 통해서 시대의 현장을 느끼듯 동시대 미술의 특성을 경험할 수 있을 것이라 생각한다. 한정된 작품을 다룬 이 글이 1990–2010년대의 미술 지형에 대한 온전한 시각을 제시할 수는 없겠으나, 전망의 단초가 되길 바란다. 아울러 이 전시를 계기로 1990년대부터 2010년대까지의 국립현대미술관의 소장품에서 아직 채워지지 않은 부분이 보완되어 실제에 가까운 전열을 갖추게 되길 기대한다.

참고문헌

국립현대미술관. 『박이소: 기록과 기억』. 과천: 국립현대미술관, 2018.
국립현대미술관. 『한국미술 1900–2020』. 서울: 국립현대미술관, 2021.
기혜경·김장언·신보슬·장승연·정현. 『한국미술 다시 보기 3: 1990년대–2008』. 서울: 현실문화, 2022.
김달진미술연구소. 『한국미술 전시자료집 III: 1980–1989』. 서울: 예술경영지원센터, 김달진미술연구소, 2017.
김달진미술연구소. 『한국미술 전시자료집 IV: 1990–1999』, 1권. 서울: 예술경영지원센터, 김달진미술연구소, 2018.
김종호, 류한승. 『한국의 젊은 미술가들: 45명과의 인터뷰』. 서울: 다빈치기프트, 2006.
김필호 외. 『X: 1990년대 한국미술』. 서울: 서울시립미술관, 현실문화, 2016
문혜진. 『90년대 한국 미술과 포스트모더니즘: 동시대 미술의 기원을 찾아서』. 서울: 현실문화, 2015.
백지숙. 『본 것을 걸어가듯이: 어느 큐레이터의 글쓰기』. 서울: 미디어버스, 2018.
(사)비영리전시공간협의회. 『도어투도어 4』. 서울: (사)비영리전시공간협의회, 2006.
윤난지. 『한국 현대미술의 정체』. 파주: 한길사, 2018.
황동일. 「종합문화공간 살바: 우리 것… 남의 것… 키치 & 고급 다 있어요」. 『한국일보』. 1997년 4월 14일 자. 21면.

이은주는 이화여대 국어국문학과와 동대학원 미술사학과 석박사를 졸업했고, 비영리전시공간 브레인팩토리의 운영자이자 독립기획자로서 인사미술공간 신진작가 지원 프로그램을 기획했다. 현재 미술사 연구와 강의, 독립 기획을 병행하고 있다. 주요 전시기획으로 《강석호: 3분의 행복》 (서울시립미술관, 2022–2023), 《Follow, Flow, Feed 내가 사는 피드》(아르코미술관, 2020), 주요 논문으로 「최후의 초현실주의 국제 전시 '절대적 거리 L'écart absolu'(1965)에 나타난 초현실적 사회상」(서양미술사학회 논문집 제58집, 2023), 「초현실주의의 현대적 신화에 나타난 공동체성: 1930–1940년대를 중심으로」(미술사학보 50집, 2018)가 있다.

Still Contemporary: Korean Art from the 1990s to 2010s

Lee Eunju
Independent curator, Art historian

백 투 더 퓨처

33

Emergence: From Collectivity to Individuality

Artists who held their first solo exhibitions between the late 1990s and the early 2000s at alternative spaces through public contests have now become the founding generation of the contemporary Korean art scene. These artists also form the central axis of this exhibition of works in the MMCA Collection, *Back to the Future: An Exploration of Contemporaneity in Korean Contemporary Art*, which attempts to identify the point at which "the context behind contemporaneity was established."[1] In the Korean art scene today, the so-called millennial and Gen-Z artists now in their 20s and 30s constitute a cultural stratum distinguished from that of the previous generation. Their new tendencies, which seemed to emerge en masse and in entanglement with one another amid rapid advancements in digital technology, went on to form a complex topography of their own. Positing contemporaneity as the characteristics of a shared (con-) timeframe (temporary)—that is, the common condition that constitutes the world of today or the holistic present and, by extension, what is considered truest to the present—to simply define contemporary art in a linear way or to pinpoint its moment of departure would be impossible at this time of cultural transition and generational shift. What may be possible, however, is to specify the point at which the visual language key to today's institution of art began to emerge, as this formed a context distinct from that of the previous generation.

Examining the titles of exhibitions held at major institution in the 1980s, such as *Actuality and Reality: '80 Painting Exhibition* (Misulhoegwan, 1980), Reality and Utterance (Dongsanbang Gallery, 1980), *Traditional Painting Today* (Kwanhoon Gallery, 1981), *The Formality of Modern Paper: Exhibition of Korean and Japanese Art* (MMCA, 1982), *Experiencing Materiality* (Gallery Jeon, Gallery Hu, 1985), and *100 Years of Korean Painting* (Hoam Museum of Art, 1986), it is evident that the concepts of "actuality," "reality," "tradition," and "materiality" underlie the shows.[2] These titles suggest that artistic discourses at the time were generated around a handful of art circles: the Minjung Art (people's art) circle, which emphasized social involvement; the Dansaekhwa (monochrome painting) circle, which pursued anti-secular and ascetic practices emphasizing materiality; the Korean traditional painting circle, which sought to modernize tradition; and the hyperrealist circle of artists, who emerged in the late 1970s through *minjeon* (exhibitions at private institutions).

Other keywords that draw attention among the titles of 1980s exhibitions centering on the themes of reality and materiality are "young," "new-generation," and "up-and-coming." While the exhibition *The Power of Korean Artists in Their 20s* (Arab Cultural Center, 1985) advocated a radical, new generation of Minjung Art, many exhibitions introduced emerging

1. Kim Hyoungmi, "Back to the Future: An Exploration of Contemporaneity in Korean Contemporary Art," MMCA.

2. Kim Daljin Art Research and Consulting, *Korean Art Exhibition Document III: 1980–1989* (Seoul: Kim Daljin Art Research and Consulting), 2017.

artists representative of new tendencies: the annual exhibition *Young Artists* (MMCA, 1981 and onward)[3], *Thing; New Generation Exhibit* (Kwanhoon Gallery, 1986), *The Spearhead in our generation* (Kwanhoon Gallery, 1987), *Exhibition of Artists in Their 30s* (Misulhoegwan, 1988), and *16 New-Generation Contemporary Artists of Korea* (Shinsegae Gallery, 1988) curated by *Gyegan Misul* (Art Quarterly) and featuring works selected by 11 critics including Seo Seongrok, Sung Wankyung, and Oh Kwang-su.[4]

These exhibitions featured artists such as Kho Nakbeom, Noh Sangkyoon, Oh Sanggil, Yook Keunbyung, Lee Bul, Cho Duckhyun, and Choi Jeonghwa— members of the 1980s artist groups TA-RA, META-VOX, Logos & Pathos, MUSEUM, and Réalité Seoul—who sought to escape the meta-discourse by proposing individuality and alternative attitudes in the face of topics related to reality and materiality.[5] Through their founding exhibitions, the group Nanjido chose to discuss "real life" over sociopolitical reality,[6] META-VOX sought to "overcome anonymized material properties,"[7] and Logos & Pathos demonstrated "the passionate creative practices of individuals,"[8] while MUSEUM presented "personal fables stemmed from a purely subjective interest."[9] These artists rose to significance in the 1990s Korean art scene, exploring reality and materiality as seen through their individual perspectives in connection to new topics such as daily life, objects, the body, and identity. Meanwhile, the "386 generation" of artists that had set out to study abroad also returned to the Korean art scene at this time, establishing an artistic language set apart from that of Minjung Art and Dansaekhwa with influences from foreign art trends.

The artistic transition toward emphasizing individuality was accelerated by the emergence of "Generation X" artists in the late 1990s. This generation had indirectly experienced the democratic movements—either orally through their seniors or through the media. With the gradual democratization that followed the Special Declaration for Grand National Harmony and Progress Towards a Great Nation of June 29, 1987, the slogans of college student protests that once rejected the authoritarian regime began to demand in-school democratization and student welfare. The opening of Korea's first McDonald's restaurant in Apgujeong-dong, Seoul, in 1988, saw the main agents of consumer culture, such as the "Orange Tribe," (a group of young, wealthy consumers that enjoyed luxury goods and fashion) congregating around the "Rodeo Streets" of Seoul. Additionally, the rock 'n' roll and folk music that once symbolized the regime-resistive youth culture gave way to songs such as Seo Taiji and Boys' "I Know," which took the country by storm immediately after the band's public TV

3. This annual exhibition, which started under the title *Young Artists* in 1981, changed its name to *Young Korean Artists* with its sixth edition in 1990.
4. Kim Daljin Art Research and Consulting, 2017.
5. TA-RA (Tabula Rasa) held its founding exhibition in May 1981, Nanjido in February 1985, META-VOX in September 1985, Logos & Pathos in August 1986, Réalité Seoul

in January 1987, and MUSEUM in February 1987.
6. Nanjido, "Our Stance," leaflet from Nanjido's first exhibition (Seoul: Kwanhoon Gallery, 1985); Kim Daljin Art Research and Consulting, *Korean Art Exhibition Document III: 1980– 1989* (Seoul: Kim Daljin Art Research and Consulting, 2017), 55.
7. Lee Il, "Preface to the Founding Exhibition," leaflet from META-VOX's

first exhibition (Seoul: Gallery Hu, 1985); ibid., 57.
8. Logos & Pathos, "Preface," leaflet from Logos & Pathos' first exhibition (Seoul: Kwanhoon Gallery, 1986); ibid., 67.
9. Yoon Jinsup, "Aggregation of Bold Expressions," leaflet from Museum's first exhibition (Seoul: Kwanhoon Gallery, 1987); ibid., 75.

debut in 1992. As reflected in the band's 1994 release "Classroom Idea," as a generation that grew up watching Hollywood films and Japanese animations and listening to J-pop, Generation X didn't necessarily resist the regime per se, but authoritarianism and uniform collectivism. With this generation, youth culture changed from a culture of student masses protesting and rallying at public squares to one of individuals meeting at and parting around consumer establishments.

As such, Generation X artists rooted their foundation in a culture substantially different from that experienced by their artistic predecessors, who sought to create fissures in the concrete discourse surrounding Minjung Art and *dansaekhwa* or the hyperrealists who debuted through minjeon. The artistic language of these artists was built on their individual idiosyncrasy—something derived from their day-to-day experiences. Whether it be the perspective of an outside observer, the sense of futility and anxiety that filled the void where collective voice used to be, the desire-inciting agent of consumer culture, or thoughts on mundane life, creating an idiosyncratic language and style soon became a prerequisite for authorship. In the absence of a central, collective aesthetic, the art of the 2000s can be seen as diversified symptoms of the individualized languages that formed, coagulated, and intertwined in response to the times.

Through the numerous "new-generation" platforms that seemed to simultaneously emerge at once in the mid-1990s, private and sporadic languages of the individualist Generation X artists were gleaned and incorporated into the institution of art to become endowed with social meaning. Artist Choi Jeonghwa's bar Sal, which opened in 1996, had art installed around the interior. There, the likes of Uhuhboo Project and PiPi Band would perform inhouse to create a hub of underground culture, art, and entertainment where artists would frequently hold exhibition afterparties.[10] Art Sonje Center, which opened in Seoul in 1998, introduced foreign art trends. Meanwhile, curator Kim Sunjung, affiliated with the center as well as SAMUSO, played a pivotal role in contextualizing the activities of Korean artists post-2000s in connection to international art trends.[11]

Regardless, alternative spaces played by far the most pivotal role. Beginning with SSamzie Space in 1998, Alternative Space Pool, Alternative Space Loop, and Project Space SARUBIA opened in 1999, followed by SSamzie Art Space and Insa Art Space in 2000. Then came second-generation spaces such as Supplement Space STONE&WATER and Space Bandee in 2002, Artspace Hue and Brain Factory in 2003, Alternative Space Team Preview in 2004, and Openspace Bae in 2006, followed by countless others including

10. Hwang Dongil, "Bar Sal: The Cultural Space that Has Everything from Korean and Foreign to Kitsch and High-End," *Hankook Ilbo*, April 14, 1997, 21. Even before Sal, there were commercial spaces that melded art with entertainment culture such as Space OJeon (opened in 1989), Baljeonso (opened in 1992), and Gompangi (opened in 1994). Quoted in Mun Hye Jin, *Korean Art of the 1990s and Post-Modernism: Tracing the Origin of Contemporary Art* (Seoul: Hyunsilmunhwa, 2015), 286.

11. Such achievements led to the exhibition *Your Bright Future: 12 Contemporary Artists from Korea* held at Los Angeles County Museum of Art (LACMA) and the Museum of Fine Arts, Houston from 2009 to 2010, co-organized by Kim Sunjung, Lynn Zelevansky, and Christine Starkman. This exhibition featured works by Koo Jeonga, Kim Beom, Kimsooja, Gim Hongsok, Bahc Yiso, Park Jooyeon, Suh Doho, Yang Haegue, Lim Minouk, Chang Younghae Heavy Industries, Jeon Joonho, and Choi Jeonghwa.

Gallery Coot, Gallery Sup, Alternative Space Miccle, and Gallery King. The launching of the NASN(Nonprofit Art Space Network), a network of alternative spaces centered around Insa Art Space in 2005 established a public funds-based system of non-profit exhibition spaces and provided support to young artists. With this, the gateway into the art scene shifted from art competitions to alternative spaces. In 2006, the network founded Artist Forum International (AFI)—with Park Chan-kyong as project director—to organize the international exhibition *Public Moment* along with projects exploring the idea of "publicness," and workshops dedicated to artist support, thereby demonstrating the network's cooperative bond.[12] This shows that alternative spaces at the time served as more than mere alternative options and had positioned themselves as an influential part of the art institution.

In the 2000s, a variety of programs that highlighted rising artists were also organized as part of an alternative effort to complement academic art school curriculums that failed to accommodate the real-art-scene experience. The most representative of these were the regional touring critique program *Door to Door* organized by the NASN in the early 2000s and Insa Art Space's program for supporting young artists, *Tool Box for Emerging Artists*. The exhibition *Yeol* curated as part of the latter went on to breed a clique of artists who debuted through the show. Furthermore, the launching of private-museum-organized art awards and public contests—such as the Hermès Foundation Art Award (2000), SongEun Art Award (2001), the exhibition *Art Spectrum* by Leeum, Samsung Museum of Art (then Hoam Museum of Art, 2001), and *the Kumho Young Artist* exhibition (2004) significantly increased opportunities for rising artists. With their debut generally accelerated, emerging artists would also enter the art market much sooner. In the years following 2005, rookie artists who garnered attention through exhibitions at alternative spaces such as Gwon Osang, Lee Dongwook, and Chung Suejin would go on to sign exclusive contracts with Arario Gallery under exceptionally generous terms and become the talk of the town. As such, the institutionalization of artist support systems led to the categorization of the individualized creative languages within the larger spectrums of diversity and experiment. Another noticeable phenomenon, is that artists began to form circles based on their exhibition venues rather than artistic tendencies.

Amid this change of various hubs forming in the gray areas between the artistic, commercial, non-profit, and public, the relationship between art and society also diversified. Minjung Art was transcribed as a chapter of history with the 1994 MMCA exhibition *Korean minjung arts: 1980–1994*, while the so-called "post-Minjung artists" inherited the resistive spirit and passed down

---

12. According to *Door to Door 4*, a sourcebook published by the NASN in 2006 at the height of the network's active demonstration of its cooperative bond, SSamzie Space, Alternative Space Pool, Alternative Space Loop, Project Space SARUBIA, Insa Art Space, Gallery JungMiSo, Supplement Space Stone & Water, Brain Factory, Space Bandee, Space Beam, Artspacce Hue, and Opensapcebae were registered as members of the council. In 2006, the council organized AFI (Artist Forum International), with Park Chan-kyong as project director to curate the large-scale international exhibition *Public Moment* along with related programs to demonstrate the council's cooperative bond. Nonprofit Art Space Network, *Door to Door 4*. (Seoul: Nonprofit Art Space Network, 2006), 97–99.

the discourse of institutional criticism through exhibitions at Alternative Space Pool, the publication of the art journal *Forum A* (1998–2005), and the editing and authoring of *BOL* (2005–2008) issued by Insa Art Space. However, the activities of post-Minjung artists often intersected with popular culture or the domain of capitalist commodities. This is clearly demonstrated by Jo Seub's strategically playful and comical works and Flying City's practical stance of questioning the capitalist urban ecology while designing a Hermès boutique window display. Park Chan-kyong, a representative post-Minjung artist and one of the administrative staff at Alternative Space Pool, won the Hermès Foundation Art Award in 2004, and was imprinted in the minds of the public as a fashionable urban elite and distinguished from his Minjung Art predecessors. This interesting visual symbolism attested to the shift in the democratization-period definition of "the avant-garde" and "practice" toward "trend" and "frontline intellect."

Progress: From Art to Visual Culture

The titles of major exhibitions of the 1990s offer an insight into how the topography of the 1990s art scene had changed dramatically from the 1980s. Titles such as *Mixed-Media* (Kumho Museum of Art, 1990), *Sunday Seoul* (Sonamoo Gallery, 1990), *Urban Pop Culture* (Dukwon Gallery, 1992), *Women: The Difference and the Power* (Hankuk Art Museum, 1994), *Man and Machine: Technology Art* (DongA Gallery, 1995), *Seoul in Media* (Seoul Museum of Art, 1996), *Apartment: An Accidental and Happy Encounter with Objects* (Gallery Artbeam, 1997), *The Visual Extension of Photographic Image* (MMCA, 1998), and *Korean Pop* (Sungkok Art Museum, 1999)[13] suggest that urban life and popular culture rose as major themes to replace social participation, anti-secularist asceticism, and nationalism. Moreover, these titles hint at the reach of feminism outside the realm of Minjung Art. Exhibitions in the 1990s were themed and formatted to better accommodate what would be referred to as "visual culture" than "art." This post-1990s progress is faithfully demonstrated by the works in the MMCA Collection featured in the current exhibition. The first recognizable aspect of the works of this period is a sense of doubt in or a call for reflection on the institution, as influenced by the conceptual and institutionally critical art of the West. In the early 1990s, Kim Beom and Bahc Yiso would distance themselves from the collective discourse, proposing criticism of and reflection on conventions and the art institution. Their perspective differed from that of Minjung artists in that it was one of a novel form of artistic agent that the Korean art scene hadn't seen before. This perspective can be seen as a result of the observant attitude the artists

13. Kim Daljin Art Research and Consulting, *Korean Art Exhibition Document IV: 1990–1999*, Vol. 1 (Seoul: Kim Daljin Art Research and Consulting, 2018), 16–118.

internalized as outcasts—during their study abroad in the United States and upon their return to Korean society—combined with the methodology of Conceptual Art.[14] Kim Beom presented viewers with situations inconsistent with their conventional expectations regarding images, to reposition them as distant observers of the very conventions. In his 1991 work *Untitled (Cooking Chicken)*, he cooked a pictorial image of a chicken according to a demonstration by a famous chef on an American TV show to induce despondent laughter and, at the same time, draw attention to the gap between a real subject and its image, nudging intellectual and skeptical reflection on canonized values.

Bahc Yiso also once described his works as a "process of justifying [his] endless doubts about everything."[15] Keeping an emotional distance in refusal to assimilate to the canonized pool of Korean men, he was cynical of the things they idolized. The intended sloppiness and fragility of the hand-crafted objects that contrast the title *World's Top Ten Tallest Structures in 2010* (2003) also reflect a futile sense of humor while neutralizing the values established by success stories and the logic of development.[16] Powered by the sense of boredom and lethargy felt towards the distant society he neither could nor wanted to be part of, Bahc endowed aesthetic form to fragility as a side effect of the "Anything is possible" attitude of the Saemaul Movement that drove Korea's compressed growth.

This attitude of indirect criticism persists in the artworks of the 2010s and beyond. A generation younger than Kim and Bahc, Koo Donghee also playfully twisted everyday contexts to betray conventional expectations. In the video work *CrossXPollination* (2016), Koo introduces two qualitatively disparate spaces—a tacky public pub and a luxurious private bathroom—under the shared theme of the desire and consumption, creating an irregular narrative structure that forces the two spaces of contrasting economic statuses and functions to gradually intertwine with each other as if to cross-pollinate two different species. This work, which refrains from stating its message till the very end, leaves a peculiar aftertaste and ultimately nudges viewers towards doubt the very conventional premises set by the artist at the beginning of the narrative. Meanwhile, Kim Sangdon, whose center of activities was Alternative Space Pool, figuratively approaches social criticism in the post-Minjung sense, incorporating highly formative objects and installations. His photo work *Monument Zero* (2014) captures a monument produced in commemoration of those sacrificed and lost due to the malfunction of public power as an alternative to the monuments dedicated to heroic figures as symbols of national ideology. Here, he embeds the socially critical message inside the

---

14. Art historian Woo Jung-Ah saw Bahc Yiso and Ahn Kyuchul to be "the forefathers of Korean discourse on conceptual art," diagnosing that "The reason these artists are doubtful about or cynical towards art's political potential despite their works consistently displaying a sense of debt toward the state and society as achieved by the '386 generation' or 'activist' elites, who finally overthrew the authoritarian military regime and realized democracy, is because they were out of the country during this time of revolution." Woo Jung-Ah, "Korean Art's Transition toward the Conceptual Post-1990," *Korean Art 1900–2020* (Seoul: MMCA, 2021), 415.

15. Bahc Yiso, "About the Works," *Bahc Yiso: Memos and Memories,* Gwacheon: MMCA, 2018, 1.

16. "Works fixed on the wall are vulnerable and ineffective, but I believe that it is for the very reason that they harbor an interestingly resistive potential, though it may not be the kind that is immediate, effective, or energetic in the face of a virtual environment." ibid., 1.

aesthetics of an artistic object as was done in the late 1990s by conceptual artists with German influences such as Gim Hongsok and Chung Seoyoung.

The second noticeable aspect is the new attitudes with which the themes of the city and daily life began to be approached. The city, which Minjung Art deemed part of the capitalist domain, begins to be introduced in artworks of the 1990s as the artists' everyday place of life. An early example of this ideology can be seen in the works of Choi Gene Uk. Despite not being featured in this particular exhibition, his works cannot be excluded from this discussion. Choi looked at the city with a sharp gaze. Deviating from the attitude of direct criticism embodied by the Minjung Art line of realists, he instead inherited the genealogy and style of hyperrealist painters, who explored urban mundanity. Through works that simultaneously reflect his sense of identity and the locality of Seoul, he managed to position himself precisely at the intersection between everyday life and painterly reality, leaning neither toward the narrative figuration of Minjung Art nor toward the technicality of hyperrealism. The ensuing generation of painters including Kong Sunghun, Kim Suyoung, Roh Choonghyun, Park Juwook, Lee Moonjoo, Lee Je, and Jung Jaeho, who went on to extend this context in the 2000s, would photograph the city as a place of their everyday life. From this, they produced paintings that convert photographic reality into pictoriality. To these artists, the city was both a place filled with potential narratives and a formative subject that needed to be soundly captured within a rectangular frame. This context is added to by the links of Kang Seokho, Park Jina, Suh Dongwook, and Lee Kwangho, who also began developing their painterly aesthetic by photographing everyday people.

Kong Sunghun, Roh Choonghyun, and Jung Jaeho's works featured in this exhibition reveal both hints of the institutional convention remaining in everyday urban landscapes and the artists' psychological dissimilation from the institution, through aesthetical devices unique to painting. Kong captures the awkwardness of the landscape of Byeokje—one that suddenly felt retrograded next to the newly redeveloped cityscape of the 2000s—and the ominous symptoms of desire that underlie it. Meanwhile, Roh's works reveal his sense of detachment from the views of the Namyeong-dong torture chamber—a remnant of state violence—and the Hangang River Park—an aspect of the cityscape that attests to the lack of design in the development—visualizing the emotional temperature with which he viewed the landscapes that had nevertheless become part of his everyday life. Jung gained recognition for his Eastern-style paintings of common apartment building façades. Highlighting the gap between the utopian blueprint of urban development and the reality of the run-down city, he filled his works with the textures of ordinary life.

Similar perspectives on the city were found in the works of video art. The 2000s saw the emergence of photographers influenced by German typological photographs, such as Keum Hyewon and Che Onejoon, who produced series of photographs capturing places symbolic of Seoul's urban system. Keum, who majored in Eastern painting, documented redevelopment sites covered with blue tarps in the series *Blue Territory* (2007–2010). Using compositions reminiscent of Eastern landscape paintings—ideal views of nature—she presents dystopian scenes in which artifacts have territorialized nature. In

Urban Depth, another serial work, Keum captured garbage disposal facilities in Seoul from a deadpan perspective to depict the city as a large and ceaseless waste-producing system.

Meanwhile, Seo Hyunsuk's video works paid attention to the gap between the architectural vision for an ideal city and the city in reality. His works were mainly critical of the urban developmental construction carried out in the process of Korea's modernization with Western modernism as its ideal. A notable example thereof is his documentary-format video *The Lost Voyage* (2011–2018) that dealt with Sewoon Shopping Center, Korea's first residential-commercial complex promoted by the Park Chung-hee regime. Through interviews and objective sources, Seo exposed the process by which Le Corbusier's ideal vision of *unité d'habitation* was transplanted into an economic development model under an authoritarian regime, prompting awareness on the real lives undermined by the glorified development plan.

The third evident aspect is the acceptance of consumer and popular cultures. Beck Jeesook, who curated the 1992 exhibition *City, Mass, Culture*, wrote in the exhibition introduction that what was required of the times was "to read more acutely into the phenomenological characteristics of popular culture and accurately grasp the idioms based on an understanding of the culture's productive side."[17] Beck's introduction recognized the dawn of the era in which art must bear the ripple effect of capitalist popular culture. On the other hand, Choi Jeonghwa, head of the Gasum Visual Development Laboratory who hybridized art and commerce from the perspective of a space designer, held a stance implicative of Korea's transition into a consumer society. Strategically exploiting the gap between the Euljiro-based subculture and the elitist aesthetic of the 1990s, her works conspicuously subsumed inexpensive and common household items as part of the art product category. In doing so, she also expanded the parameters of art. As proposed by Min Joungki's deliberate incorporation of kitsch into 1980s Minjung Art, Choi optimized the communicative potential of subculture within the context of a consumer-based society. Embodying such duality, Choi's works offer a vivid look into the symptoms of the era in which consumer culture infiltrated the realm of art.[18]

Meanwhile, Lee Dongi chose to work with and tweak popular and iconic images over subjective ones. Through this approach, he attempted to visualize his status as part of the first generation of artists that grew up exposed to consumer culture. First presented in 1993, the character Atomaus symbolizes the identity of the generation that grew up watching *Astro Boy* and *Mickey Mouse*. Lee once mentioned that there is no originality to his works and that

17. Beck Jeesook, "City, Mass, Culture," *City, Mass, Culture*, exhibition catalog, Seoul: Dukwon Gallery; Beck Jeesook, *Walking Across the Seen: Writing Explained by a Curator* (Seoul: Mediabus, 2018), 28.
18. In this context, art historian Yun Nanji pointed out that Choi Jeonghwa's works share aspects of pop art in that they parody capitalism but the addition of

signifiers of indigenous culture, that is, "vernacular" elements differentiate them from pop art. Yun Nanji, "Choi Jeonghwa's Plastic Semiotics," *The Identity of Korean Contemporary Art* (Seoul: Hangilsa, 2018, 577–578). Art historian Shin Chunghoon also remarked that Choi's works are "closer to kitsch or vernacular art than impassive pop art in that they harbor narratives and are

psychologically stimulating," adding that they can be interpreted as "an allegory of the unstable nature of Korea's compressed modernization and an ode to aesthetic potential of the anonymous designs produced in the age of urbanization and industrialization." Shin Chunghoon, "The Public Life of Korean Art Post-1990s," *Korean Art 1900–2000* (Seoul: MMCA, 2021), 383.

he aspires "to be an artist who does not create anything."[19] Mirroring this attitude, his work *Man and Woman* (1990) features a man and a woman, who have been erased of existential weight and converted into images that are similar to the superficial symbols circulated around consumerist society.

The fourth mentionable aspect is the exploration of video media. In the 1990s, a decade marked by the transition from analog to digital, video artists went on to expand the boundary of video art as set by their predecessors by combining it with installation or experimenting with the specificity of advanced media. In the early 1990s when video was an unfamiliar medium to the Korean art scene, Lee Yongbaek was one of the first to attempt to conflate video with other media such as sculpture and installation, and experiment with computer-based video editing techniques, cleverly exploiting the dynamic between the mise-en-scène and the viewer's perspective. A statement on the panic that ensued the financial crisis of 1997, *Vaporized Things (Post IMF)* produced between 1999 and 2000 is remarkable not only for its conflation of performance and video media but also in that viewers' experience of the video—which lies somewhere between immersion and observation— ultimately becomes part of the work itself. In the early 2000s, Ryu Biho effectively melded video media's characteristic, mechanical coldness with an institutionally critical perspective. Produced through technical editing, his work *Black Scud* (2000) features black silhouettes of virtual figures engaging in an endless running motion yet failing to get anywhere. The figures' uniform gestures overlap with the image of the crowd in the last scene and are reminiscent of animals in captivity, thereby sending an implicit message.[20]

Meanwhile, Kim Sejin paid attention to the temporality of video as a digital medium. In *Reverse* (1998), she presents a narrative that retrogresses the flow of physical time to explore the theme of temporality using a method unique to the freely editable video medium, deeming video art the art of time. In this work, teardrops shed by a woman travel back up to defy gravity then begin to be shed anew, and the looped sequence is endlessly repeated. Using editing techniques to reverse and repeat a moment and stretch it into what feels like an eternity, Kim creates a non-linear and psychological space-time akin to memory. Park Hwayoung captures a stray dog in a semi-documentary format in *Jaywalker* (1998), by inserting a virtual scene in which she communicates with the solitary dog, Park completes a narrative unique to video as the fictional and non-fictional obtain equal senses of reality. Based on a documentary capturing real-life circumstances faced by a fiction filmmaker, Ham Yangah's *fiCtionaRy* (2002–2003) also delves into the relationship between fiction and non-fiction as a condition inescapable by video. The insertion of behind-the-scenes footage from the actual shooting of the video reminds viewers that creating fiction, to a filmmaker, is an existential experience that entails forging relationships with actors as real subjects, not virtual ones.

19. Kim Jongho and Ryu Hanseung, *Young Korean Artists 45: Interviews* (Seoul: DaVinci Gift, 2006), 142.
20. This type of critical view of the capitalist system led to reflection on media. Ryu Biho and Yangachi's joint exhibition *Public Cell* (2002) sought to raise awareness on the dangers of the media system, likening it to Big Brother for controlling and brainwashing the masses.

The art world's acceptance of the communication method of the video-culture generation in the 2000s gave rise to "new media art" including internet-distributed forms of web art. In 2000, Roh Jaeoon exhibited his works through the website vimalaki.net and ideated web art that viewers could voluntarily access via their personal computers with a simple scroll. In this work, produced using postproductions of clips from classic films, the narrative is determined by viewers and the order in which they choose to click on the clips. This work is significant in that it proposed a new method of communication tailored to the age of one-person media.[21]

New media works of the 2010s often dealt with the body—its status in between reality and virtual reality—amid the familiarization of digital media. They also dealt with the phenomenon of immaterial data occupying physical "storage space" within the digital world. For example, Kim Ayoung, a representative artist utilizing new media in the present progressive sense, has explored the migration of data within the digital space in connection to the issues of global migration, territory, and power through the series *Porosity Valley*. Her critical view on power is also evident in her early work *PH Express* (2011), which dealt with the tension created among the Western powers over Geomundo Island. The 2010s also saw the emergence of realistic-virtual images produced with 3D graphic programs that blurred the line between reality and virtual reality. A prominent example is Kim Dujin's *Moses, Dying Slave, Victory* (2016–2017), in which the ideal images of Michelangelo's iconic works disintegrate into myriad pieces of decaying bones as the viewer approaches the work.

The fifth notable aspect is the reaction to globalization. With MMCA Gwacheon's hosting of the Whitney Biennial in 1993 and the Venice Biennale's opening of the Korea Pavilion in 1995, links began to form between Korean art and the contemporary flow of international art. By the 2000s, young Korean artists could be commonly found working abroad as part of various residency programs, and their reaction to globalization can be sensed through works produced post-2000s in their exploration of cultural transition. Though excluded from this exhibition, Park Jooyeon's *MONOLOGUE monologue* (2006), in which the voice of a Korean student reading in English is synched over the image of a native English teacher, depicts the process through which the dominant culture is transmitted and disseminated. Similar consciousness can be read from works of the 2010s. Nam Hwayeon has produced works that trace the context underlying conventional concepts and images since the mid-2000s, among which the 2017 work *Throbbing Dance* reads into the social context underlying the body. The three women featured in this work each formulaically practice dance moves from the Hollywood movie *Flashdance* then unite to perform a group dance. The work encourages viewers to question whether these movements are, then, an expression of freedom or an assimilated

21. Roh Jaeoon stated that he came to create the website vimalaki.net while communicating with musicians, writers, and cartoonists, adding that viewers can choose to see the website itself as a work of art, appreciate the individual works on the website, or create their own work by selecting and editing the list of works. Kim Jongho and Ryu Hanseung, ibid., 58.

form of popular value. This shows how the movements of a female in a typical American film are adopted and reinterpreted as a political group dance under the name "throbbing dance" in North Korea, and again as a dance manual for young women in South Korea. Ultimately, the work demonstrates how the ideology of the body is transferred and translated differently depending on varying cultural contexts.

On the other hand, An Jungju's *Drill* (2005), which likens Chinese police officers' chanting of slogans during a close-order drill to a percussion performance, shows how the ideology of a society can be interpreted merely in terms of style and sound from a tourist's view. An also produced *Hand in Hand with Amigos para Siempre* (2016) during his stay in Barcelona, in which the official theme song for the Barcelona Olympics "Amigos Para Siempre" and the theme song for the Seoul Olympics "Hand in Hand" were remixed and edited in with the broadcast footage. By means of dismantling the integrated narrative, the work hinders viewers' immersion into the larger agenda of globalization propagated by the songs, and creates a psychological distance that neutralizes the hyperbolized and ideal message.

Overviewed thus far—and focusing on the exhibited works from the MMCA Collection—is the flow of art from the late 1990s and 2000s marked by the emergence of Generation X to the subsequent tendencies of the 2010s. From the current point in time, marked by the anticipated and dreaded infiltration of artificial intelligence into daily life, the 1990s and the 2000s may feel like a distant past. However, the visual languages conceived during this period are inherently contemporary in that they are still undergoing an evolution in reaction to present-day phenomena. It was during the 1990s that I began taking an interest in contemporary art as a graduate student studying art history. And in the 2000s, I became an active member of the Korean art scene as a curator and critic. Understanding that what we consider chapters in history today were all once an intricate web of events triggered by tension and passion at the frontline of the scene, I recognized just how limited historical narratives are. Nevertheless, as it is my duty to establish a perspective and imbue shape to the tendencies that seemed only erratic at the time, I have but to persistently attempt to narrate the past. As suggested by the title *Back to the Future*, this exhibition retrogresses chronological time in a time-traveling manner to offer an almost on-scene experience of the characteristics of contemporary art. Centering only on a limited number of works, this essay couldn't possibly fully map the topography of Korean art from the 1990s to the 2010s, but I hope it marks the beginning of the prospect. I also hope, with this exhibition as an opportunity, that the MMCA's collection of works from the 1990s to the 2010s is complemented with works from previously omitted parts of history to constitute a truly comprehensive compilation.

References

Beck Jeesook, *Walking Across the Seen: Writing Explained by a Curator.* Seoul: Mediabus, 2018.

Nonprofit Art Space Network, *Door to Door 4*, Seoul: Nonprofit Art Space Network, 2006.

Hwang, Dongil, "Bar Sal: The Cultural Space that Has Everything from Korean and Foreign to Kitsch and High-End." *Hankook Ilbo*, April 14, 1997, 21.

Ki, Heykyung et al., *Rethinking Korean Art 3: 1990s–2008*, Seoul: Hyunsilmunhwa, 2022.

Kim Daljin Art Research and Consulting, ed., *Korean Art Exhibition Document III: 1980–1989*, Seoul: Kim Daljin Art Research and Consulting, 2017.

Kim Daljin Art Research and Consulting, ed., *Korean Art Exhibition Document IV: 1990–1999*, Vol. 1, Seoul: Kim Daljin Art Research and Consulting, 2018.

Kim, Jongho, and Hanseung Ryu, Young *Korean Artists 45: Interviews*, Seoul: DaVinci Gift, 2006.

Kim, Pilho et al., *X: Korean Art in the Nineties*, Seoul: Seoul Museum of Art, Hyunsilmunhwa, 2016.

Mun, Hyejin, *Korean Art of the 1990s and Post-Modernism: Tracing the Origin of Contemporary Art*, Seoul: Hyunsilmunhwa, 2015.

National Museum of Modern and Contemporary Art, Korea, ed., *Bahc Yiso: Memos and Memories*, Gwacheon: MMCA, 2018.

National Museum of Modern and Contemporary Art, Korea, ed., *Korean Art 1900–2020*, Seoul: MMCA, 2021.

Yun, Nanji, *The Identity of Korean Contemporary Art*. Paju: Hangilsa, 2018.

Lee Eunju received Ph.D. in Art history at Ewha Womans University. She worked as an supervisor and curator of the non-profit art space Brain Factory. She planned and launched a incubating program for young artists as an associate curator of the Insa Art Space. She is currently conducting research and lectures on contemporary art history, as well as independent curating. She curated the exhibitions including *Three Minute Delight* (Seoul Museum of Art, 2022–2023), *Follow, Flow, Feed* (Arko Art Center, 2020), Published the papers including *The Vision of Surreal Society in the Last International Surrealist Exhibition 'L'écart absolu' (1965)* (*Journal of the Association of Western Art History* 58, 2023), *Communality Manifested in the 'Modern Mythologies' of the Surrealists in the 1930s and 1940s* (*Korean Bulletin of Art History* 50, 2018)

역사에서
대중 소비사회로,
공동체에서 각자도생으로

'지금'
1990년대는
무엇이었나

함돈균

문학평론가

역사의 종언과 1990년대

모든 연대기는 앞선 시대의 카르마이자 잔영이며, 다음 시대의 준비이자 예고편이다. 10년 단위의 연대기는 자연적 시간의 흐름 속에 역사적 차원의 인식론적 단절을 도입하려고 하나, 이 지층에는 이전 연대기의 역동이 고스란히 남아있다. 이 역동은 강진 이후 찾아오는 여진이라기보다는 시그널로 시작되어 지형 전체를 삼켜버리는 쓰나미와 같다. 증후는 증폭되고 마침내 풍경으로 보편화된다. 그러므로 연대기적 단절이란 인식론적 착시이다. 하나의 연대기는 갑작스러운 불연속단층면이 아니라 오히려 팬데믹이라고 해야 한다. 최초에는 병자가 마스크를 썼으나, 이후에는 시나브로 마스크를 쓰지 않는 자가 범법자가 되는 낯선 풍경을 마주하게 되는 것이다.

1989년에 미국의 정치학자 프랜시스 후쿠야마(Francis Fukuyama)가 『내셔널 인터레스트』(The National Interest)에 발표한 논문 「역사의 종말」(The End of History)은 1980년대의 마지막 시점에서 1990년대의 시작을 예측하는 논쟁적 주장이었다. 그는 1990년대 이후의 세계를 이념적 쟁투가 진행되어 온 근대 인류 전체의 역사적 운동이 종결된 시대로 본다. 근대 세계에서 자유주의(자유민주주의)와 내내 대결해온 파시즘, 전체주의, 공산주의 이념의 패배는 인정투쟁에 의해 진행되어 온 역사의 전진 운동이 완결되었음을 뜻한다. 1990년대는 자유주의 이념에 의해 완성된 역사, 그러므로 종결된 승리의 역사로 진입하는 관문이며, 여기에서 더 이상 경쟁해야 할 이념이나 추구할 만한 대의명분이 없는 인간들은 삶의 의미를 찾아 방황하는 최초의 '종말인'이 된다.

후쿠야마의 역사종말론이 선언될 무렵인 1989년은 11월에 있었던 베를린 장벽의 붕괴로 마감되었으며, 1990년대는 1990년 10월에 있던 서독의 동독 흡수 통일로 시작되었다. 그리고 이듬해인 1991년, 자유주의 이데올로기와 경쟁했던 사회주의의 모체 소비에트연방이 해체되기에 이른다. 1990년대의 기본 지형이란 20세기 세계사의 이념적 운동이 종결(?)되었다는 차원에서 파악될 수밖에 없다. 문명사가 유발 하라리(Yuval Harari)는 이를 '거대한 이야기'의 종말이라고 표현한다. 세계사적 이념 쟁투의 종속 변수로 탄생했던 20세기 분단국가 한국에 이 상황은 더 특별한 함의를 지녔다. 분단체제의 한국사회에서 좌파적 이념은 국가 파시즘 진영과 민주화 운동 진영 모두에게 필요한 양날의 칼로 작용해왔기 때문이다. 정부 수립 이래 전체주의적 사회 통제를 근간으로 국가를 운영하던 1990년대 이전의 대한민국 정부는 공산주의 이념의 위험성을 적극적으로 선전하는 반공주의 전략을 통해 사회를 통치해왔다. 민주화 운동 세력은 이에 맞서 좌파의 진보적 이념을 의식적으로든 무의식적으로든 사회운동과 역사의 비전을 그려내는 중요한 동력으로 활용해왔다.

그러나 서구와는 달리 세계전쟁의 여파가 나은 기형적 분단체제로 출발한 대한민국은 이 불구적 상황 탓에 보다 복잡한 사회이념적 갈등을 내포한 사회가 될 수밖에 없었다. 1940년대 해방정국에서 공존했던 사회이념적 지형, 즉 박헌영의 민중주의와 이승만의 자유주의, 여운형의 좌우합작론과 김구의 민족주의 노선이 경쟁하는 이념적 내전 상태를 사실상 1980년대 중후반까지 줄곧 지속해 올 수밖에 없었던 것이다. 1987년 시민항쟁에 의한 대통령직선제 쟁취는 이런 이념적 갈등의 일정한 해소 계기가 될 수 있는 것이었지만, 민주화 운동의 역사적 과실을 온전히 쟁취하지 못한 대통령 선거의 결과는 불행히도 한국의 정치사회 체제를 온전히 1990년대로 진입하지 못하게 했다. 이즈음 동시적으로 진행된 세계사적 이념 및 체제 전쟁의 종결은 한국의 민주화 운동이 더 이상 역사의 방향성에 어떤 '외부' 가이드라인도 가질 수 없는 현실이 도래했음을 뜻하는 일이었다. 하지만 이 상황은 막 시작된 1990년대 한국사회에 냉전적 이념 내전 상황을 완화해 준 것이 아니었다. 오히려 분단체제 하의 한반도는 1990년대에 이르러 세계사에 유일한 냉전국가로 남아있게 되었다고 해야 할 것이다. 다시 말해 1990년대의 한국에서 역사는 종말에 이른 것이 아니라, 전진도 후퇴도 아닌 기묘한 착종 상태에서 '비정상성의 정상성'을 공고화하는 새로운 현실로 접어들었던 것으로 보인다. 1980년대의 마지막에서 1990년대를 예감했던, 그리하여 1990년대에 가장 많은 사랑을 받았던 시인 기형도의 유고 시집은 이즈음의 풍경을 이렇게 적었다. "이곳은 처음 지나는 벌판과 황혼/내 입 속에 악착같이 매달린 검은 잎이 나는 두렵다"[1]

거대한 보수주의의 출현과 반복되는 1980년대

1990년대의 정치사회 구조가 만들어지는 과정은 흡사 프랑스혁명이 시민봉기 이후 반동적 정치 쿠데타를 통해 복고주의 왕정으로 회귀하는 것과 비슷한 인상을 주었다. 1987년의 시민봉기가 대통령직선제 쟁취를 통해 역사의 일정한 전진을 이루어내는 것처럼 보였으나, 오히려 신군부 세력을 대표하는 인물에게 통치권의 정당성을 이양하는 이벤트가 되면서, 시민들의 내적 분노는 더 격렬해졌고 회한은 더 깊어졌다. 정치사회적 불안은 가라앉지 않았고, 1989년도에는 분노한 노동자들의 대궐기가 일어났다. 선거를 통해 정권을 잡기는 했으나 도덕적 정당성이 애초에 허약했던 노태우 6공화국 정부는 정치적 불안감을 일거에 해소하기 위해 1990년대에 들어서자마자 사실상 거대한 '보수 쿠데타'라고 할 만한 일을 마치 군사작전처럼 단행했다. 1990년대 한국사회에 대한 구조적 이해는 물론이고, 지금까지 한국사회의 기본적 토대를 이해하는 데에 핵심이 되는 사건이 바로 1990년 1월에 있었던 '민주자유당'의 창립이다. 민주자유당의 창립은

---

1. 기형도, 「입 속의 검은 잎」, 『입 속의 검은 잎』
   (서울: 문학과지성사, 1989).

한국사회의 정치사회적 장기 구조 변동을 기획한 정치 이벤트라는 점에서 흔히
보는 정치인들의 이합집산과는 차원이 다른 사건이었다. 민주자유당의 창립은
1960년대 이래 군사파시즘과 유신체제를 대표하는 인물과 1980년대 신군부체제를
상징하는 인물과 그에 맞선 민주화운동 세력의 상징적 인물 간의 연합이라는
점에서 상상하기 어려운 종류의 일이었다.

이 연합의 현실적 결과는 분명하고 파괴적이었다. 1990년대가 되었지만 여전히
과거 군사 파시즘에 뿌리를 둔 매머드급 냉전 보수정당이 출현했다. 서로 다른
세력 간의 연합은 진영 간 경계를 흐림으로써 우리 사회 구성원들을 판단의 혼란
속으로 몰아넣었다. 그리고 거대 보수정당은 실제로 1990년대 한국사회에 완고한
보수주의 흐름을 만들어냈다. 이 보수주의는 철저한 지역 분할 전략에 기초해
있었다는 점에서 퇴행적이었으며, 국가를 분열시키는 효과를 만들어냈다는 점에서
보수주의의 전통적 의제인 '공동체주의'와도 다른 수구적 성격을 띠는 것이었다.
세계사적 이념 쟁투가 극적인 종말을 맞고 있는 시점에서 한반도의 냉전 상황과
지역주의를 정치 이벤트로 적극 활용한 이 사건은, 1990년대가 낳은 가장 결정적인
이념 구조 변동에 관한 사건이며, 이 효과는 지금까지 존속되고 있다. 2023년의
대한민국은 1990년대의 산물이기도 한 것이다.[2]

이러한 반동적 성격의 보수주의 구조화에 따라 한국사회의 민주화 운동은
1990년대가 들어서도 여전히 격렬한 사회저항 운동, 유사 재야운동의 성격을
띨 수밖에 없었다. 1989년 결성되어 대규모 해직사태를 맞아 재야운동이 되고만
전국교직원노조의 장외투쟁이 1990년대 중반까지 격렬하게 전개되었고, KBS의
방송 민주화 운동이 그런 양상을 띠었으며, 명지대생 강경대 치사 사건으로
촉발되어 무려 11명의 분신자살로 이어진 1991년도의 분신 정국이 그러했다.
전투적 노동운동이 거리와 사업장에서 정부와 치루는 전쟁처럼 진행되는 등
1990년대 중반까지 한국사회는 후쿠야마 식 이념시대의 종결과는 전혀 다른 시대
양상을 보였다. 1980년대가 연장된 것 같은 이 정치적 혼란상은 1987년 시민항쟁이
지닌 미완결성의 결과인 동시에 한국사회 민주화의 역사적 흐름에 반격을 가한
1990년대 발 보수대연합의 반동적 효과이기도 했다. 이 보수대연합은 1990년대
후반 한국사회가 국가부도 사태라는 비상 상황에 직면하여 헌정사상 선거에 의한
최초의 정권 교체가 이루어지기까지 극심한 사회적 저항과 위태로움 속에서도
가까스로 지탱되었다.

---

2. '민주자유당'의 창립에 관한 기본적
   시각은 강준만의 저서를 참조했다.
   강준만, 『한국 현대사 산책 1990년대편 1』
   (서울: 인물과사상사, 2006).

영화 산업, 대중문화를 통한 현실의 재인식과 감각의 개방

전체주의적 통제를 본질로 하는 1990년대의 정치적 반동 보수주의 흐름은 사회 전반에 도덕주의적 캠페인의 양상으로 나타나기도 했다. 그것은 노태우 정부에서 '범죄와의 전쟁' 선언으로 표현되었다가, 이후 문민정부가 출현한 뒤에는 문민성의 표현으로서 더 선명한 도덕주의 캠페인으로 나타났다. 그러나 이러한 사회문화적 도덕주의가 전체주의적 통제에 기초해 있다는 사실은 대중문화에서 창작의 자유를 제한하는 각종 심의 및 검열 제도, 예컨대 음반과 영화에 관한 사전검열제가 여전히 유지되고 있는 현실 속에서 그 허구성을 드러낼 수밖에 없었다. 소설 『즐거운 사라』로 외설 논쟁을 일으킨 연세대학교 교수 마광수가 강의 도중 구속되고(1992) 대학교수직에서 결국 해직되었으며(1996), 비슷한 이유로 작가 장정일이 『내게 거짓말을 해봐』로 실형을 선고받고 법정 구속되는(1997) 등 1990년대 중반이 되고 문민정부가 출현했어도 사회 통제의 기조는 크게 바뀌지 않았다.

그러나 정치적 통제를 통해 사회의 역동성을 완전히 가둬두는 일은 불가능한 일이다. 1990년대에는 풍속적 도덕주의 흐름이 해체되어 가는 사회문화적 증후가 여기저기서 뚜렷하게 나타나기 시작했다. 이 해체적 흐름에 가장 중요한 축을 형성한 것은 대중문화였다. 다양한 문화적 저항과 취향. 장르 분화 현상이 나타났으며, 이 현상 속에서 본격적으로 대중문화의 산업화·자본화가 이루어졌으며, 이미 축적된 대자본이 문화 시장에 적극 개입하는 양상이 나타났다.

이 글은 이 시대의 분위기를 뚜렷이 드러내는 몇 가지 사례에만 집중해 보려고 한다. 우선 영화산업을 언급하지 않을 수 없다. 1990년대는 한국영화가 '방화'라는 이름으로 폄하되던 지난 시대를 벗어나 진정한 의미의 씨네필이 생겨나고 자기 정체성을 구축하기 시작한 시대였다. 1980년대 가장 많은 관객을 동원한 상위 영화들의 상당수가 에로티즘을 소재로 한 작품들이었지만, 1990년대 관객동원 상위 10위권에는 '에로 영화'가 없었다.[3] 1980년대 방화의 주된 종류였던 에로 영화는 군사 파시즘 정부가 국민들의 불만을 다른 것으로 돌리기 위해 조장한 외설 전략의 부산물이었던 동시에, 전체주의적 사회 통제를 위해 필요한 풍속 도덕주의의 희생양으로서 정권이 유지·관리해야 하는 존재라는 이중적 성격을 지녔다. 그러나 임권택의 「장군의 아들」(1990), 「서편제」(1993)로부터 초유의 흥행 성과를 올리며 1990년대를 연 한국영화는 점차 전통적 한의 정서나 민족주의적 이데올로기에서도 벗어나 변화하는 시대적 분위기와 풍경 및 감수성을 담는 작품들을 선보였다. 이 과정에서 다양한 스타일과 영화적 자의식을 지닌 감독들을 대거 출현시키고

3. 1980년대 최고 흥행작 10편은 다음과 같다. 「깊고 푸른 밤」(배창호, 1985), 「매춘」(유진선, 1988), 「고래사냥」(배창호, 1984), 「어우동」(이장호, 1985), 「미워도 다시 한번 80」(변장호, 1980), 「애마부인」(정인엽, 1982), 「자유부인」(박호태, 1981), 「이장호의 외인구단」(이장호, 1986), 「무릎과 무릎 사이」(이장호, 1984), 「서울무지개」(김호선, 1989). 한편 1990년대 최고 흥행작 10편은 다음과 같다. 「쉬리」(강제규, 1999), 「서편제」(임권택, 1993), 「주유소 습격 사건」(김상진, 1999), 「투캅스」(강우석, 1993), 「편지」(이정국, 1997), 「약속」(김유진, 1998), 「텔미 썸딩」(장윤현, 1999), 「장군의 아들」(임권택, 1990), 「접속」(장윤현, 1997), 「인정사정 볼 것 없다」(이명세, 1999). 김경욱, 「1990년대 한국영화 장르의 스펙트럼」, 『1990년대 한국영화』(서울: 앨피, 2022).

발군의 배우들을 성장시켰다. 또 시장에서의 상업적 성공과 대중의 문화적 욕구에
고무된 전문 투자자 및 대기업의 자본 투입을 통해 한국영화 시장의 산업화가
본격적으로 시작되었다.

임권택으로 시작된 1990년대 한국영화 르네상스는 박광수, 장선우, 이명세, 강우석,
강제규, 홍상수, 이창동, 허진호 등 개성과 흥행력을 겸비한 다수의 감독들을
출현시켰으며, 이는 한국영화 글로벌 시대를 연 박찬욱(「JSA 공동경비구역」,
2000)과 봉준호(「살인의 추억」, 2003)의 2000년대를 예비하는 시간이었다.
이들의 개성들은 각기 달랐던 바 박광수의 리얼리즘적 문제의식은 「아름다운 청년
전태일」(1995), 「이재수의 난」(1999) 등 역사적 사실의 영화·드라마적 도입으로
수용되었으며, 장선우는 논쟁적 사회이슈들을 매번 도발적인 장르문법으로
실험했다. 「남부군」(각본. 1990), 「우묵배미의 사랑」(1990), 「화엄경」(1993),
「너에게 나를 보낸다」(1994), 「꽃잎」(1996), 「나쁜 영화」(1997)는 모두 영화적으로
뿐만 아니라 사회적으로도 이슈를 만들어냈다. 「나의 사랑 나의 신부」(1990)로
1990년대를 흥행감독이란 수식어로 시작한 이명세는 1990년대 말 「인정사정 볼 것
없다」(1999)에 이르러 대중영화를 장르 고유의 극단적 미학 실험으로 승화시키면서
작가주의로 나아가려 했다. 홍상수는 「돼지가 우물에 빠진 날」(1996), 「강원도의
힘」(1998) 등을 통해 일상의 도덕주의와 지식인의 허위의식을 까발리는 낯선
질문과 독특한 편집 방식 및 시나리오 작성법을 선보이면서 1990년대 이후 한국적
작가주의 탄생의 선명한 시그널이 되었다.

한편 「초록물고기」(1997), 「박하사탕」(1999), 「오아시스」(2002)로 이어진 이창동의
서사의식은 역사와 삶의 실제를 직시하는 정직한 성찰에 근거해 있었으며,
「8월의 크리스마스」(1998)에서 보여준 허진호의 따뜻한 영화적 감수성은
2000년대 「봄날은 간다」(2001)를 통해 한국적 멜로드라마의 새로운 꽃을 피운다.
「투캅스」(1993)로 1990년대를 열고 「공공의 적」(2002)과 「실미도」(2003)로
2000년대로 건너간 강우석은 공권력을 소재로 한국형 시리즈 흥행물을 창안했고,
「은행나무 침대」(1996)로 우뚝 서서 「쉬리」(1999)로 1990년대를 마무리한 강제규는
한국형 블록버스터 시장을 만들어내고 영화투자방식의 혁신을 이끌면서 한국영화의
대중화와 산업화에 크게 기여한 것으로 평가된다.[4] 이러한 감독의 영화들은 시대
반영적 성격이 강하고 엔터테인먼트 산업이면서 거대 자본을 필요로 하는 영화
장르의 특성상 1990년대 한국사회의 변화상을 여러 층위에서 압축적으로 반영하고
있었다.
미학적 자의식을 지닌 1990년대 한국영화 감독들의 도전과 만개는 관객들로 하여금
대중미디어를 통해 현실을 재인식하게 하는 소격 효과를 발생시켰다. 할리우드
규모의 영화산업 시스템이나 기술력, 자본시장, 소비시장을 확보하고 있지 못했던

4. 장병원, 「리얼리티의 발견, 모더니티의 도래」,
    「1990년대 한국영화」(서울: 앨피, 2022)
    참조.

1990년대의 한국영화는 영화적 현실을 애초부터 판타지로 설정하는 할리우드식 전략이 아니라 사회적 현실과 일정한 관련성을 지닌 미학적 가상을 통해 또 다른 현실로 나아가려는 독특한 역동성을 지니고 있었다. 이는 정치적 보수주의와 풍속적 도덕주의를 거절하는 대중문화의 저항 방식인 동시에 대중미디어산업이 크게 확장되는 산업자본화 과정이기도 했다. 영화산업의 활력으로 인해『씨네21』, 『키노』같은 영화전문지들이 1995년에 창간되고, 한국예술종합학교에 영상원이 설립되었으며(1995), 부산국제영화제(1996), 부천판타스틱영화제(1997)를 비롯하여 한국은 여러 개의 국제영화제를 가진 보기 드문 아시아 국가가 됨으로써 1990년대는 '한국적' 대중문화의 폭발적 확장에 중요한 분기점이 되었다. 이는 한국사회를 이념의 사회에서 대중문화의 시대로 전환하는 데에 큰 영향을 끼쳤다. 1980년대 거리에서 사회운동의 이념을 외쳤던 젊은이들이 대거 영화산업과 영화 담론으로 몰리기도 했으며, 씨네필들은 영화에서 사회운동의 대안과 비전을 보기도 했다.

1990년대 한국 영화산업의 발전은 당시 영화인들에게 큰 저항적 이슈가 되었던 할리우드 영화 직배시스템 도입과 「쥬라기공원」(1993) 쇼크로 상징되는 할리우드 블록버스터의 상업적 공포가 야기한 자연스러운 문화적 산업적 응전 현상이기도 했다. 한편 글로벌 자본력과 기술력을 지닌 할리우드 영화산업의 공습은 한국인들의 대중문화 소비 욕구를 강하게 건드렸고, 이 수요를 흡수하기 위한 멀티플렉스 상영관들이 들어서면서 서울과 도시의 전통적 극장가들은 이들로 대체 되기 시작했다. 동네 가까운 곳에 들어선 멀티플렉스라는 안락한 극장의 출현은 영화를 일상 소비문화의 일부로 받아들이게 했다. 이러한 흐름과 더불어 편의점 수만큼이나 동네 곳곳으로 급속히 퍼져나갔던 비디오 대여점은 대중들의 생활에 보이지 않는 감각의 변화를 촉진하고 있었다. 영상미디어의 아카이브이자 보급로였던 비디오 대여점은 1990년대를 사는 사람들의 미디어 감각을 급격히 문자문화에서 영상문화로 이동시켰으며, 일상 시간을 일정하게 영상미디어들의 향유로 채우는 라이프스타일의 전환 및 재배치를 촉진했다. 여가시간을 OTT 서비스에 내어준 오늘날 한국 도시인들의 보편적 라이프스타일은 이즈음부터 리뉴얼되기 시작했다고 해야 할지도 모른다.

취향의 연대, 신세대와 서태지

세계사적 이념전쟁의 종말은 이념의 상실이 아니라 실은 보수주의 이데올로기의 독점적 지배를 뜻하는 것이었다. 한국 사회운동의 관점에서 그것은 '글로벌' 가이드라인의 상실이었고, 내부적으로 완결되지 못한 민주화운동의 결과는 사회운동들의 성격을 여전히 1980년대에 머물도록 강요했다. 그러나 1990년대에는

1980년대 사회 변화의 주역으로 불린 386세대(1960년대생, 80년대 학번)와는 다른
세대가 성장하고 있었으니, 대학가는 이제 1970년대생의 시대였던 것이다. 그들이
들어온 대학은 1980년대의 잔영이 남아 있었으나, 이미 그때와는 다른 시대 지형에
놓여 있었다. 무엇보다도 그들은 이념을 소유하는 것이 아니라, '감각'을 소비하고
문화를 향유하는 사회 지형에 놓여 있었다. 1980년대를 떠나보내고 1990년대를
맞이한 386세대에게 가장 큰 충격은 반동적 거대 보수주의 정치 지형의
재등장이었지만, 1990년대 '신세대' 학번들에 가장 큰 쇼크는 1992년 등장한
서태지와 아이들(이하 서태지)의 데뷔였다. 1집 「Seotaiji and Boys」(1992)는
쇼크였으나, 2집 「하여가」(1993)에서 그 쇼크는 열광으로 바뀌었으며, 3집 「발해를
꿈꾸며」(1994)와 4집 「컴백홈」(1995)에서 서태지는 이미 사회과학의 분석 대상이
되어 있었다. 1집은 데뷔 앨범으로는 역대 최다인 180만 장이 판매되었고, 서태지는
그해 한국의 모든 대중가요 시상식을 휩쓸었다. 2집은 220만 장이 판매되었고,
이 앨범은 대한민국 100대 명반에 선정되었다. 3집은 160만 장이 판매되었으며
서태지는 학계와 언론계가 선정한 '광복 50년 한국을 바꾼 50인'에 가수로서는
최초로 선정되었고, 「교실 이데아」는 고등학교 교과서에 수록되었다. 4집은 발매
첫날만 30만 장, 총 240만 장이 판매되었다.

서태지는 가사, 리듬, 선율 등 음악을 이루는 모든 요소와 무대매너, 의상, 미디어
및 대중 소통 방식 등 쇼비즈니스를 이루는 다양한 요소에서 시대적·산업적 이슈를
만들어냈으며, 아주 영리한 방식으로 시대와의 불화조차 상업화하는 압도적인
능력을 발휘했다. 1990년대는 물론이고 한국 대중문화 역사상 가장 강력하고
성공한 이슈메이커였던 그들은, 1990년대 젊은이들로 하여금 '대중문화'에 속한
음악의 '소비'를 통해 시대를 함께 살고 유쾌하게 저항한다는 묘한 일체감을
불러일으켰다. 서태지는 아직 1980년대의 연장선상에 머물러 있던 1990년대 초의
사람들, 특히 젊은이들의 생의 감각을 이전 세대와 완전히 갈라놓은 핵폭탄급
크랙이었다. 1990년대의 사회적 저항이 이전 시대와 가장 다른 점은 서태지로
대표되는 대중문화 아이콘에 대한 대중의 향유 감각이 곧 연대일 수 있다는 '취향
공동체' 의식이 나타나기 시작했다는 점일 것이다. 1990년대의 '신세대'는 더 이상
이념 서적을 읽지 않는다. 그들은 취향으로 '연대'한다(고 느낀다).
서태지의 엄청나게 예외적인 성공은 그가 1990년대 신세대 대중문화를 가르는
적어도 3개의 층위를 절묘하게 분유했기 때문이다. 홍대의 인디문화는 서태지
좌파라고 할 수 있다. 텔레비전으로 대표되는 공중파 방송 쇼비즈니스 팬덤은
서태지 우파라고 할 수 있다. 특별한 분류라고 할 수 있지만 괄호에 넣을 수도
없는 시대적 증후로서 압구정 오렌지족 문화는 서태지가 발산하는 이미지의
어떤 극단적인 부분과 닿아 있다. 그들은 서태지 외전이다. 1990년대를 이해할
때 홍대를 중심으로 한 인디문화, 서브컬처의 성장도 주목할 만한 일이지만,
산업적인 관점에서는 공중파 쇼비즈니스 팬덤으로 분류되는 서태지 우파의 영역이
대중문화의 강력한 소비자로 부상한 10대로 주축을 이뤘다는 점도 주목을 요한다.

서태지가 자극하여 1990년대 중반 이후 등장한 1세대 아이돌그룹, 예컨대 H.O.T와 같은 1세대 아이돌 팬덤의 주요 주체와 동력은 이제 확실히 구매력을 갖춘 10대였다. 그 시장은 1990년대에 SM엔터테인먼트, 대성기획(현 디에스피미디어), YG엔터테인먼트 등의 전문 음악기획사 체제의 설립으로 이어지고, 2010년대 이후 만개하여 한국 대중문화 글로벌 산업화의 기초가 되었다.

민방, 몸, 접속, 라이프스타일

이즈음에서 이 시기 대중미디어 환경의 변화를 기억하는 일은 매우 중요하다. 1991년 민영상업방송 SBS의 출범은 텔레비전 시대의 진화를 촉진하는 특별한 사건이었으며, 이 영향은 현재 수많은 종합방송채널 시대의 등장만큼이나 지대한 것이었다. 공영성을 희석한 민영상업방송의 출현으로 시청자의 소비 감각에 초점을 맞춘 드라마와 쇼들의 제작이 양적으로나 질적으로 촉진되었다. SBS의 출현으로 전속계약제가 해지된 상황 속에서 탤런트들의 타방송국 이동이 촉진되었고 방송사 간 시청률 경쟁이 격화되었다. 방송 토크쇼 전성시대가 열렸으며, 1990년대의 독보적인 라이징 TV 스타 최진실이 탄생했고, 광고가 드라마처럼 진화했으며, 아니 드라마가 광고의 포맷을 추종했으며, 텔레비전 드라마와 광고가 삶을 디자인하는 '라이프스타일' 시대가 본격적으로 시작되었다.[5]

정치권력의 통제 대상이었던 '몸'은 후기자본주의가 가장 주목하는 '몸-상품'으로 전환되면서 노골적으로 시장과 광고의 중심 오브제 및 상품이 되었으며, 그에 따라 소비 대상으로서의 자기 신체에 대한 폭발적 관심이 대중에게 일어났다. 뷰티 산업, 성형 산업, 바이오헬스 산업이 본격적으로 시작된 것이다. 「질투」(1992) 같은 트렌디 드라마가 등장했으며, 트렌디 드라마의 현실을 대중은 자신의 현실로 욕망했고, 최진실의 광고 문구가 제안하는 라이프스타일이 새로운 인생 가이드가 되었으며, 이를 소비로 충족하지 못하는 시청자들은 자신의 현실을 결핍의 현실로 인식했다. 궁핍의 시대가 막 지나가자 행복과 불행은 절대적 빈곤의 문제가 아니라 소비 충족에 관한 상대적 결핍감의 문제가 된 것이다. 바야흐로 1990년대는 소비 욕망 시대의 티핑포인트였다.

1995년 시작된 케이블TV 시대와 지역 민방 시대의 출범은 이러한 흐름을 더욱 가속화했다. 패션, 자동차, 아파트, 직업, 중산층, 강남, 신용카드, 땅, 주식, 벤처. 1990년대의 중후반을 넘어서면서 가장 빈번히 사람들의 입에 오른 내린 '기호'들이다. 1980년대를 겨우 견디고 1990년대로 건너간 이 땅의 사람들은 정치적 주체로서 '시민'이 되기보다는 소비의 주체로서 '소비 대중'이 되고

5. 이에 관한 자세한 정황은 주 1 참고할 것.

있었다. 시민사회로의 역사적 이력을 거친 후 후기자본주의 사회로 이행한 서구의 경우와는 달리, 한국사회는 1970–1980년대의 민중 담론 이후 '시민'을 건너뛰고 바로 '소비대중사회'로의 급격한 이행을 준비하는 듯이 보였다. 정이현의 소설집 『낭만적 사랑과 사회』(2002)는 1990년대 라이프스타일의 주체들이 어떤 '몸'을 형성하게 되었는지를 보여주는 도시인류학적 보고서인데, 이 소설에서 주인공 '나'는 뉴비틀과 루이 비통, 샤넬백을 소유하기 위해 자신의 '몸'을 관리하며, '순결'을 도덕적 문제가 아니라 상품 전략으로 기획하는 교환의 주체로 등장한다. 시인 유하는 일찍이 이 풍경을 1990년대 초입에서 "사과맛 버찌맛 온갖 야리꾸리한 맛, 무스 스프레이 웰라폼 향기 흩날리는 거리/웬디스의 소녀들, 부티크의 여인들, 카페 상류사회의 문을 나서는 구찌 핸드백을 든 다찌들"[6]로 요약한 바 있다. 1980년대의 사람들은 1990년대가 되면 가난에서 벗어날 뿐만 아니라 보다 평등하고 민주화된 사회에서 이웃과 더불어 행복한 삶을 증진시킬 수 있을 것이라 기대했으나, 어느덧 욕망의 기호로 둘러싸인 1990년대의 삶에서 행복은 상대적 결핍의 문제가 되었으며, 서로를 물질적 기준으로 견주어 보는 의식 속에서 불행의식은 오히려 더 커진 듯이 보였다. 2023년 UN의 글로벌 이니셔티브인 '지속가능한 발전 해답 네트워크'(Sustainable Development Solutions Network)가 발간한 「세계행복보고서」(World Happiness Report)는 한국의 행복지수를 OECD 국가 중 최하위인 57위라고 발표했는데, 물질의 성장과 삶의 만족도가 반비례하는 지표 아이러니가 한국사회에서 감지되기 시작한 것은 1990년대부터라고 해야 할 것이다.

1990년대 이전의 한국인들은 '정권 교체'가 세상을 획기적으로 바꿔놓을 것이라는 신념으로 역사에 헌신하거나, 적어도 그런 믿음을 '뜨겁게' 가슴에 품고 살았으나 1990년대와 이전 세계를 확연히 갈라놓은 것은 정치적인 이슈가 아니라 예상치 못한 '쿨한' 뉴미디어의 등장이었다. 장윤현 감독의 영화 「접속」(1997)은 이런 관점으로 1990년대 '모던 로맨스'의 새로운 풍경을 압축적으로 그려낸 흥행작이었다. 사랑의 상처를 안고 있는 익명의 두 남녀가 PC통신으로 대화하면서 자기 화해를 거쳐 결국 실제 '접속'에 이르는 과정을 그린 이 영화는 얼굴 없는 만남이 가능해진 뉴미디어 시대의 소통 방식을 인상적으로 보여주었다. PC통신은 단순히 접속자 간 대화를 넘어서 PC통신문화라고 하는 독특한 공론장 문화를 만들어냈는데, 천리안·하이텔·유니텔 등의 PC통신 게시판은 취향의 공동체를 이루며 다양한 사회문화적 식견을 게시하고 논쟁하는 새로운 담론문화의 장이 되었다. 일반 대중과 시민의 의견이나 관점·리뷰·논평 등을 널리 공유할 수 있는 장이 없었으며, 공론장이라곤 사회적으로 공인된 식자층이나 전문가집단에만 허용된 전통적 신문과 잡지밖에 없었던 사회에서, 이는 관점의 다원주의와 말의 민주주의를 개방하는 획기적인 공간의 출현을 뜻했다. 또 PC통신은 시공간을

---

6. 유하, 『바람부는 날이면 압구정동에 가야 한다』(서울: 문학과지성사, 1991).

초월한 정보 유통을 가능하게 했다. 그리고 이러한 온라인 문화는 1998년 김대중 정부에 의해 세계에서도 가장 선제적으로 도입한 초고속 인터넷망의 국가 차원의 신설을 통해 2000년대 포털 붐의 초석이 되었다.

인터넷의 출현은 라디오, 텔레비전의 발명 이상으로 혁명적인 미디어의 출현을 의미하는 것이었으며, 1980년대와 그 이후의 시대를 어떻게 구분할 수 있을까 하는 지점에서 핸드폰의 등장과 더불어 가장 혁명적인 사건이라고 할 수 있다. 1990년대로부터 불과 20–30년 만에 한국이 세계 무대에서 경쟁력 있는 국가로 부상하게 된 가장 중요한 요인이 무엇일까. 그것은 문민정부 시절 추상적인 캐치프레이즈로 남발되었던 레토릭으로서의 '세계화'가 아니라, 바로 이 시점에 신속하게 도입된 초고속인터넷망의 설치를 통해 '디지털 국가'로의 결정적인 계기를 마련했다는 사실에도 있지 않을까.

새천년인가, 세기말인가

세계사적 이념전쟁의 종말과 정치적 보수주의의 득세에도 불구하고 경제적 호황과 대중문화의 산업적 확장, 소비문화에 대한 대중적 욕구가 폭발하며 양적·질적 팽창을 하는 것처럼 보이던 한국사회는, 그러나 1997년 국가 채무불이행 선언함으로써 그 이전 시대의 사회경제적 토대나 사회적 이상과는 완전히 결별한 듯 준비도 되지 않은 채 돌이킬 수 없는 '세계화'의 흐름 속으로 갑작스레 빨려 들어갔다. 산업자본주의에서 금융자본주의로의 세계적 이행 현상 속에서 발생한 '국가 부도' 사태, 그리고 그 해결책으로 IMF와 맺은 구제금융협약은 그 이전 민주화 운동의 역사적 과정 속에서 한국인들이 열망했던 인권의 보편화나 공동체적 자유의 이념과는 아무런 연관이 없었다. 프란시스 후쿠야마는 자유주의의 승리를 역사의 종언이라고 했지만, IMF를 통해 강요되고 수용된 금융자본주의의 '글로벌 스탠다드'는 사회의 공동체적 안전망을 해체하는 방향으로 진행되었으며 역사의 (이념이 아니라) '이상'을 아예 지워버렸다.

특히 IMF는 고용시장에 자유경쟁체제 도입을 강제했고, 상당수 노동 유형을 계약직과 비정규직으로 전환할 것을 종용했으며, 그 결과 기존 한국사회의 평생직장 개념은 순식간에 해체되었다. 그리하여 상시적 고용불안과 '실업사회'가 구조화되었다. 또 IMF는 전기·가스·수도·철도·의료 등 사회공공재 및 사회서비스에 대한 민영화 요구를 강제적으로 관철시켰다. 김대중 정부는 국민들의 '고통 분담' 덕에 만 4년이 지나지 않아 IMF 구제금융 체제를 벗어났다고 선포했으나, 구제금융 체제 이후의 한국사회는 더 이상 이전과 같은 사회가 아니었다. IMF에 의해 관철된 세계화로의 편입은 한국사회의 분위기와 공동체적 감성을 완전히 바꾸어 놓았고 '파괴'했다.

총량으로서의 물질적 부가 증대하고 대중문화가 산업적으로 의미 있는 규모로
팽창하고 다채롭게 번성했던 1990년대였지만, 그것은 한편 공동체적 전망과
연대감을 거세하는 방향으로 나아가고 있었다. 각자도생을 전술로 삼는 우리 시대
개인들의 생존 중심 멘탈은 1990년대 말 IMF 체제를 통해 이식된 세계화 체제의
산물이라고 볼 수 있다. 연대의 이상이 거세된 세계에서 더 이상 전진할 방향도
방법도 의욕도 없는 존재가 된 이들은 각자의 섬에 고립되었고, 각자의 방에
갇혔으며, '광장'과 '역사'를 잃었다. 모두가 정글 속에 던져져 있다고 느꼈다(느끼고
있다). 그 고립감과 불안과 허무의 틈새로 세기말의 '밀레니엄 콤플렉스'가
엄습했다. 다행인지 불행인지 시계가 2000년 0시를 알렸지만 밀레니엄 버그는
없었으며, 휴거도 일어나지 않았다.

그러나 그로부터 20여 년이 지난 지금, 그 세기말의 공포는 또 다른 사회현상으로
변이되고 증식하여 회귀하고 있는 것은 아닌가. 2023년 현시점에서 한국의
정신문화 및 대중문화 현상을 관찰할 때, 눈에 띄는 일 중 하나는 급속도로 번지고
있는 유사 종교의 '소비' 현상이다. 예컨대 전통적 기독교 교단을 대체하는 듯이
세력을 키워나가는 '새로운' 기독교 종파. 중국을 통해 들어온 종래 전통 불교가
아니라 서구를 거쳐 수입된 인도불교 및 명상에 대한 대중의 폭발적 관심. 다양한
유사 종교 및 신흥 종교, 개인 신앙, 영성 산업의 활황. 이러한 추세는 인류문명이
심각한 위기를 맞닥뜨리고 있는 현재 공통으로 목격되는 '글로벌' 현상이지만,
한국의 경우 이 현상이 퍼져나가는 추세는 더 빠르고 깊숙하며 넓어 보인다. 혹시
이 현상은 IMF 이후 공동체적 황량함 속에 경험했던 1990년대 발 밀레니엄
콤플렉스의 심리적 씨앗이 개화한 불안의 연꽃은 아닌가. 만일 그렇다면 호흡을
가다듬고 '지금 이 순간'에 집중한 이 시대의 명상 수행자(소비자)들은 '지금
여기'의 실체를 이렇게 감지할지도 모른다. 이 세기가 새천년의 시작이 아니라
종말의 세기일 수도 있다는 사실 말이다. 그리하여 1990년대를 관찰하며 다음
세기를 예감한 한 '디지털 명상가'는 이 시대의 '영성'에 관해 다음과 같은 예언을
남겨 두었던 것이다.

"몸 속에 웹 브라우저를 내장하게 되었어. 야금야금 제 속을 파먹어 들어가는 달.
신이 몸 속에 살게 되었어. 신은 이제 몸 속에서 키울 수 있는 존재야."

"2000년 5월 11일 오후 1시 같은 종족인 s와 나는 유목 물품을 파는 대형 소핑몰의 입구에서
만난다 겨울 유목지로 이동할 s와 나는 신들의 축목과 유목 물품이 필요하다."[7]

7. 이원, 『야후!의 강물에 천 개의 달이 뜬다』 중에서
    (서울: 문학과지성사, 2001).

함돈균은 문학평론가, 문명비평가, 러닝 디자이너로
고려대, 이화여대, 한예종 등 많은 대학에서 문학과 철학,
예술론 등을 강의해 왔으며, 문체부, 교육청, 서울시민대학,
서울문화재단, 삼성전자, 리움미술관, 플라톤아카데미 등에서
새로운 인문·예술 교육프로그램을 디자인하고 자문해 왔다.
파주타이포그라피학교 인문연구소장, 고려대 민족문화연구원
HK연구교수, 시민행성 대표, 현대자동차 헤리티지북
프로젝트 초대 편집장을 지냈다. 현재 제주 독립책방
시타북빠와 어반스피리추얼 컴퍼니 다스딩 대표이며, 명지대
문예창작학과 객원교수이다. 『사물의 철학』『순간의 철학』 등
10여 권의 책을 냈다.

From History to a Mass Consumer Society, from Community to "Everyone for Themselves":

What Were the 1990s "Now"?

Hahm Donkyoon
Literary critic

The End of History and the 1990s

All chronologies represent the karma and after image of the preceding era, as well as a preparation for and preview of the era to come. Chronologies based on ten-year units attempt to introduce an epistemological break at the historical level into the natural flows of time, but the dynamism of the previous era lingers within each subsequent decade. This dynamism is less like an earthquake's aftershock, more like a tsunami—starting out as a signal and comes to engulf the entire terrain. The symptoms are amplified until they eventually become a universal landscape. The chronological break is thus an epistemological illusion. Instead of appearing as a sudden and discontinuous fault line, a chronology is more akin to a pandemic. First, you see only sick people wearing masks; eventually, you find yourself in an unfamiliar landscape where those who do not wear masks are viewed as criminals.

"The End of History?," a 1989 article published in *The National Interest* by the US political scientist Francis Fukuyama, made a controversial argument that predicted the beginning of the 1990s in the final moments of the 1980s. He saw the 1990s and onward as an era that would see the end of modern historical movements for all of humankind, which up till then, had been the subject of fierce ideological battles. The defeat of ideologies that had been consistently at odds with liberalism (liberal democracy) in the modern world— fascism, totalitarianism, and communism—signified the completion of history progressing only in the face of struggles for recognition. The 1990s were a gateway into a history completed by liberal ideology, a history of concluded victory. Thus, people of this generation would be the first of the "last people," wandering about in search of the meaning of life without any more ideologies to compete over or causes to pursue.

Fukuyama's declaration of the end of history came in 1989, a year that ended with the collapse of the Berlin Wall in November; the 1990s were rung in with West Germany's absorption of the East in October. A year later in 1991, the very matrix of the socialism that had been battling with liberal ideology—the Soviet Union—began to disintegrate. The basic topography of the 1990s could only be interpreted in terms of the "end" of the ideological movements of the modern era and the 20th century in particular. Civilization historian Yuval Noah Harari has called this the end of the "grand story." This situation holds special implications for Korea, a nation whose 20th-century division emerged as a subordinate variable to an ideological battle within world history. Under the division regime, leftist ideology in South Korea has operated as a double-edged sword, essential for state-fascist and democratization campaigners alike. Pre-1990s South Korean regimes ruled the state through totalitarian social controls. The government held society in their grip through an anti-communist strategy that actively propagandized the dangers of communist ideology. Against this, forces campaigning for democratization both consciously and unconsciously used left-wing, progressive ideology as a key driving force for devising social movements and historical visions.

Starting as it did from a different place than the West—that is, from a skewed division regime spawned by the aftereffects of a world war—South Korea found itself trapped in a position where societal development could only occur while harboring complex social and ideological conflict. In other words, it inevitably sustained the same social and ideological terrain that coexisted from the post-liberation years of the 1940s, until more or less the mid-to-late 1980s. This philosophical civil war pitted Pak Honyong's populism in competition with Rhee Syngman's liberalism, Lyuh Woonhyung's calls for left-right collaboration, and Kim Koo's ethnic nationalism. The achievement of a direct presidential election system through a citizens' uprising in 1987 was able to put some of this ideological conflict to bed. However, the results of the presidential election showed a failure to fully reap the historical fruits of democratization and were unfortunately unable to usher South Korea's political and social systems fully into the 1990s. The "end" of the global battle over ideology and regimes happening around the same time signified that South Korea's democratization movement now faced a reality where it could no longer depend on any "external" guidelines for the direction. Even so, the situation at the beginning of the 1990s did not quiet the Cold War-era ideological civil war in South Korean society. The divided Korean Peninsula therefore somewhat represents the only remaining "Cold War countries." History had not ended in late-1990s South Korea; instead, it appeared to have entered a new reality where the "normality of the abnormal" became further entrenched in a curious entanglement without advancement or retreat. The landscape around this time was described in a posthumous collection by Gi Hyeong-do. A most beloved poet of the 1990s, Gi predicted the decade from the vantage point of the end of the 1980s: "I pass this wilderness, this twilight, for the first time/ I'm afraid of the black leaf sticking stubbornly in my mouth" ("Black Leaf in My Mouth," *Black Leaf in My Mouth*, 1989).

The arrival of big conservatism and the repetition of the 1980s

The formation of political and social structures in 1990s South Korea is reminiscent of the situation after the French Revolution, where a citizens' revolt was followed by a reactionary political coup and a return to a revivalist monarchy. The citizens' uprising in 1987 seemed to have achieved some historical progress with the institution of a direct presidential election system. Instead governing power was transferred to someone who represented the "New Military Forces" that had ruled during the dictatorship. Inwardly, the public's rage intensified, and regrets deepened. The political and social turmoil did not subside, and by 1989 angry workers were holding large-scale rallies. The Sixth Republic administration Roh Taewoo had come to power through an election, but its moral legitimacy was fragile from the outset. In an attempt to quickly clear away the political anxieties, it undertook what amounted to a military operation as the 1990s commenced—what might be called a grand "conservatism coup d'état." This incident, which is key to understanding the structure of South Korean society in the 1990s and the basic foundation of society as it has continued until today, was the founding of the Democratic

Liberal Party in 1990. In terms of its being a political event intended to achieve a shift in the long-term political and social structures of South Korean society, the Democratic Liberal Party's foundation was a different matter entirely from the sorts of shifting alliances so often seen among politicians. It was an unimaginable sort of business, in which one figure who had represented military fascism and the Yushin regime since the 1960s united with another who symbolized the New Military Group regime of the 1980s, and yet another who symbolized the democratization movement against them.

The practical results of this alliance were obvious and devastating. It ushered in a mammoth Cold War-era conservative party, which remained rooted in the military fascism of the past. By blurring the boundaries among the different camps, this diverse alliance left the members of South Korean society at large plunged into confusion. This big conservative party would go on to establish a current of staunch conservatism in South Korean society during the 1990s. But this was a regressive form of conservatism, in that it was rooted in a strategy of thorough division among regions. Taking on a reactionary aspect, it stood separated from conservatism's traditional "communitarianism" agenda in that it had the effect of dividing the nation. At the same time that global ideological struggles were coming to a dramatic end, this development actively and politically exploited the Korean Peninsula's Cold War-era situation and regionalism. This incident marked the most decisive ideological shift of the 1990s, and its effects continue to this day. The South Korea of 2023 is also a product of the 1990s.[1]

In the face of this reactionary conservatism, the South Korean democratization movement was obliged to continue an intense campaign of social resistance—a partially-dissident movement—even in the 1990s. Formed in 1989, the Korean Teachers' and Education Workers' Union (KTU) was forced into dissident movement status after large-scale terminations, and it continued its intense struggle into the mid-1990s. The KBS network's broadcasting democratization movement took on a similar role, and the year 1991 was marked by a number of self-immolations following the death of Myongji University student Kang Kyungdae, with no fewer than 11 people taking their lives by setting themselves on fire. With a combative labor movement waging a veritable war against the government in streets and workplaces, the South Korean society of the mid-1990s was in a very different historical place from the "end of ideology" described by Fukuyama. This state of political confusion which seemed to prolong the 1980s, was a product two things: the incompleteness of the 1987 citizens' uprising and the conservative, 1990s grand alliance that followed and struck back against the historical current of democratization in South Korea. That alliance would be precariously sustained amid extreme social resistance up until South Korea's first-ever election of an opposition administration in the late 1990s while South Korea was faced with the crisis of a national default.

1. For the basic perspective on the establishment of the Democratic Liberal Party, I referred to Kang Joonman, *A Walk Through Korean Contemporary History: The 1990s, Vol. 1* (Seoul: Inmul, 2006).

Reperceiving Reality and Opening the Senses through the Film Industry and Popular Culture

The political current of reactionary conservatism in the 1980s, with its essential focus on totalitarian control, also manifested in the form of moralistic campaigns across society. First expressed by the Roh Taewoo administration with its declaration of a "war on crime," such movements became more defined as an expression of "civilianness" following the arrival of the Kim Youngsam presidency (which became known as the Munmin Jeongbu, or "civilian administration"). This social and cultural moralism was rooted in totalitarian control, and the falseness of its pretexts was revealed in a reality where creative freedoms in popular culture were still restricted by censorship and review systems, including prior censorship applied to musical recordings and films. Yonsei University professor Ma Kwangsoo was arrested during one of his classes in 1992 after his novel *Happy Sara* became the focus of an obscenity controversy; in 1996, he was finally fired from his position as a university professor. The writer Jang Jeongil was sentenced to prison time and taken into court custody on similar grounds for his novel *Try Lying to Me* in 1997. Even by the mid-1990s with the arrival of the Kim Youngsam administration, the climate in terms of social control had not changed much.

However, it was beyond the ability of any political controls to completely cage society's dynamism. During the 1990s, clear signs were appearing throughout society and culture suggesting that the old-fashioned morality was breaking down. Perhaps the most important element in this disintegration was popular culture. Various phenomena of cultural resistance, taste, and genre differentiation emerged and acted as a catalyst that saw popular culture undergoing a full-scale shift toward an industry—and capital— based model. The accumulation of massive stores with large capital became actively involved in the culture market.

For this essay, I want to focus on just a few of the examples that clearly illustrate the social climate at the time. First of all, it is necessary to mention the film industry. The 1990s was a decade when South Korean cinema left behind its *banghwa* (a term referring to "national cinema," but with pejorative connotations of relative shoddiness), and saw the emergence of cinephiles in a true sense as well as the first establishment of its own identity. While many of the 1980s top-ranked films—in terms of audience numbers— had to do with erotic subject matter, none of the top ten best-performing films in the 1990s fell into the "titillation" category.[2] Such titillating films had been one the main

---

2. The 10 highest-earning Korean films of the 1980s were: *Deep Blue Night* (Bae Changho, 1985), *Prostitution* (Yu Jinseon, 1988), *Whale Hunting* (Bae Changho, 1984), *Eoh Wu-Dong* (Lee Changho, 1985), *Love Me Once Again Despite Hatred '80* (Byeon Jangho, 1980), *Madame Aema* (Jeong Inyeop, 1982), *Liberal Wife* (Park Hotae, 1986), *Lee Changho's Baseball Team* (Lee Changho, 1986), *Between the Knees* (Lee Changho, 1984), and *Seoul Rainbow* (Kim Hosun, 1989). The top 10 highest-earning films of the 1990s were: *Shiri* (Kang Jegyu, 1999), *Seopyeonje* (Im Kwontaek, 1993), *Attack the Gas Station* (Kim Sangjin, 1999), *Two Cops* (Kang Woosuk, 1993), *The Letter* (Lee Junggook, 1997), *A Promise* (Kim Yoojin, 1998), *Tell Me Something* (Chang Yoonhyun, 1999), *General's Son* (Im Kwontaek, 1990), *The Contact* (Chang Yoonhyun, 1997), and *Nowhere to Hide* (Lee Myungse, 1999). Kim Gyeonguk, "The Genre Spectrum of 1990s Korean Cinema," *Korean Cinema of the 1990s* (Seoul: Ipbook, 2022).

forms of *banghwa* during the 1980s, and were the by-product of a strategy by the fascist military regime. Using obscenity to divide public satisfaction the films also took on the secondary role as something the regime needed to sustain and manage as a scapegoat of the traditional moralism needed for totalitarian control. But as the 1990s began with the unprecedented box office success of director Im Kwontaek's films such as *General's Son* (1990) and *Seopyeonje* (1993), South Korean cinema began to transform. Shifting away from the traditional sentiments of *han* (bitterness) and ethnic nationalist ideology it instead reflected the changing historical climate, landscape, and sensibilities. This process led to the emergence of numerous directors with varied styles and cinematic awareness, while also nurturing outstanding actors. Meanwhile, the commercial success of such firms and the public's increased demand led to funding from professional investors and large-scale businesses and the subsequent full-scale development of the South Korean film market into an "industry."

The 1990s South Korean film renaissance that began with Im Kwontaek would go on to produce numerous directors who combined individuality with profit-drawing popularity, including Park Kwangsu, Jang Sunwoo, Lee Myungse, Kang Woosuk, Kang Jegyu, Hong Sangsoo, Lee Changdong, and Hur Jinho. The period also offered a preview of the 2000s and the filmmakers who would usher in South Korean cinema's global era, including Park Chanwook (*Joint Security Area*, 2002) and Bong Joonho (*Memories of Murder*, 2003).

The directors each exhibited their own individual approach: Park Kwangsu's realist critical stance was incorporated in the dramatic adoption of historical subject matter in films such as *A Single Spark* (1995) and *The Uprising* (1999), while Jang Sunwoo addressed controversial social issues in his experiments with different the provocative forms of genre structure (*North Korea's Southern Army*, 1989; *The Lovers of Woomook-baemi*, 1990; *Passage to Buddha*, 1993; *To You, from Me*, 1994; *A Petal*, 1996; *Bad Movie*, 1997). After starting the 1990s as a director of commercially successful films with *My Love, My Bride* (1990), Lee Myungse made a move toward auteurism by the end of the decade with *Nowhere to Hide* (1999), elevating the popular film through the extreme aesthetic experimentation characteristic of the genre. Hong Sangsoo deployed unique editing techniques and screenwriting approaches alongside odd questioning that laid bare everyday morality and the false consciousness of intellectuals in films such as *The Day a Pig Fell into the Well* (1996) and *The Power of Kangwon Province* (1998). The 1990s clearly signaled the emergence of a South Korean model of auteurism.

Meanwhile, the narrative consciousness displayed in the films of Lee Changdong—from *The Green Fish* (1997) to *Peppermint Candy* (1999) and *Oasis* (2002)—was grounded in an honest reflection on the truth of history and life, and the warm cinematic touch that Hur Jinho brought to *Christmas in August* (1998) would lead to the emergence of a new form of Korean melodrama in the 2000s with *One Fine Spring Day* (2001). Starting the 1990s with *Two Cops* (1993) and moving into the 2000s with *Public Enemy* (2002) and *Silmido* (2003), Kang Woosuk developed a South Korean model for series with commercial appeal while focusing on examples of authority figures. Kang Jegyu, who distinguished himself with *Ginkgo Bed* (1996) and rang out the 1990s with *Shiri*

(1999). Kyu is believed to have greatly contributed to the popularization of South Korean film and the development of the industry with his creation of a market for South Korean blockbusters and his guiding role in innovations in film investment methods.[3] The directors' films are strongly reflective of their times, and due to the nature of film as an entertainment industry that requests huge capital investments, they also offered brief and varied reflections of the changes South Korea underwent in the 1990s.

The risk-taking and blooming of South Korean film directors boasting aesthetic self-awareness in the 1990s had an alienating effect on viewers, prompting them to perceive their reality anew through the lens of popular media. At the time, South Korean cinema did not boast a Hollywood-scale film industry system or enormous technical capabilities and capital and consumer markets. Instead, it assumed a unique form of dynamism. In place of the Hollywood strategy that positioned cinematic realities as fantasy from the outset, it sought to move toward a reality that, through aesthetic imagination, bore some connection with the real-world social environment. This was simultaneously a form of popular-culture resistance that rejected political conservatism and traditional morality, and a process of developing a capital-driving industry as popular media underwent huge expansions. The vitality of the film industry led to the establishment of such film journals as *Cine 21* (1995) and *Kino* (1995). Also in 1995, a school of film was created in the Korea National University of Arts. South Korea became the rare example of an Asian country hosting numerous international film festivals, including the Busan International Film Festival (created in 1996) and Bucheon International Fantastic Film Festival (1997). In this way, the 1990s represented a major turning point in the explosive expansion of South Korean popular culture. This would have an enormous influence on the transition from a society of ideology to a popular culture society. The same young people who advocated for social movement ideologies on the streets in the 1980s began moving en masse toward the film industry and film discourse, while cinephiles saw the alternatives and visions for social movements that were present in films.

The development of the South Korean film industry in the 1990s was also an example of culture and industry fighting against the introduction of the direct Hollywood film distribution system (an issue that sparked massive resistance from film professionals at the time) and the commercial threat of Hollywood blockbusters, as symbolized by the seismic impact of *Jurassic Park* (1993). Meanwhile, the onslaught waged by the Hollywood film industry with its global capital and technical capabilities tapped strongly into South Koreans' desire to consume popular culture. To absorb this demand, multiplex cinemas opened up and began to replace the traditional theater districts of Seoul and other cities. The advent of conveniently-situated multiplex theaters in multiple neighborhoods led people to adopt film as part of their everyday consumer culture. Alongside this trend, the rapid proliferation of video stores—which

3. See Kim Gyeonguk and Jang Byeongwon's "The Discovery of Reality and Advent of Modernity," ibid.

became about as ubiquitous as convenience stores—also began stoking subtle sensory changes in the public's lives. As archives and distribution channels for video media, these stores quickly shifted the media perceptions of people living in the 1990s from written culture to moving image culture, precipitating a lifestyle transition in which people filled a certain amount of their daily lives with such media. Perhaps we may conclude that the lifestyle of South Korean urbanites—those who give their leisure time over to streaming services today—began to change around this period.

Taste Solidarity: The New Generation and Seo Taiji

The "end of ideological warfare" in world history did not, in fact, signify a loss of ideology but rather a monopoly of conservative ideology. From the perspective of South Korean social movements, this was the loss of a "global guideline," and the failure of the democratization movement to reach internal completion forcing social campaigns to remain stuck in the 1980s. The 1990s, however, saw the coming of age of a generation different from the so-called "386 Generation" (South Koreans born in the 1960s who entered university in the 1980s), the members of which had been cited as the key instigators of social change in the 1980s. The universities already belonged to 1970s babies. They arrived in institutions where the afterimages of the 1980s still lingered, but the historical landscape they occupied was already different from before. Most crucially, they were placed in a social terrain of consuming "perceptions" and enjoying rather than subscribing to ideologies. The biggest shock to the system for the 386 Generation as they bade farewell to the '80s and entered the '90s was perhaps the reemergence of a large reactionary/conservative political landscape. The biggest shock for members of the new generation entering university in the 1980s was the 1992 debut of the musical act Seo Taiji and Boys. Their self-titled debut album in 1992 set off shock waves in its own right, but with the second album's single *Anyhow Song* (1993), those waves developed into a craze. By the time their fourth and fifth albums were released—boasting the singles *Dreaming of Balhae* (1994) and *Come Back Home* (1995) respectively—they were already the subjects of sociological analyses. The first collection sold 1.8 million copies, the most ever for a debut album. The act went on to sweep the honors at that year's popular music award ceremonies. The second album sold 2.2 million copies and has been named one of the top 100 South Korean records of all time. The third album sold 1.6 million copies, while Seo Taiji became the first singer named in a list of "50 people who changed South Korea" selected by scholars and journalists in celebration of the 50th anniversary of Korea's liberation. The song *Classroom Idea* was included in high school textbooks. The fourth album sold 300,000 copies on the first day of its release and 2.4 million in total.

Seo Taiji and Boys created historical and industry issues in terms of all the different elements that went into music (lyrics, rhythm, melody, and so forth) as well as those in show business (stage manner, outfits, ways of communicating with the media and public). The group showed a masterful ability to cannily commercialize everything—right down to its conflicts with the times. As the most powerful and successful trendsetters not just of the 1990s but of South Korean popular culture history as a whole, the members led the 1990s youth to experience a curious sense of oneness as they shared a historical moment and an exhilarating form of resistance through the consumption of popular music and culture. For South Koreans still caught in the hangover of the previous decade, the band had an almost nuclear impact in terms of completely separating young people's worldviews from those of the previous generation. That which distinguished the social resistance of the 1990s from the previous era the most, was the first emergence of a "community of taste": the idea that popular enjoyment of cultural icons (Seo Taiji and Boys) could itself be a form of solidarity. The new generation of the 1990s no longer read ideological texts. They united (or perceived themselves as uniting) through taste.

Seo Taiji and Boys' enormous and exceptional success lay in the way they subtly distinguished at least three different sectors of the new generation's 1990s popular culture. The indie culture around Hongik University in Seoul could be described as the "Seo Taiji left." The "Seo Taiji right" would be the show biz fan base consuming publicly broadcast media, especially television. The so-called "Orange Tribe" (a group of young, wealthy consumers that enjoyed luxury goods and fashion) culture centering on Seoul's Apgujeong-dong was a historical symbol that could also be seen as a special category, albeit one that may be placed in parentheses; in any event, it touched upon certain elements at the extremes of the Seo Taiji and Boys image. They could be called the "Seo Taiji spin-offs." The indie culture around Hongik University and the development of subcultures are notable in terms of understanding the 1990s. But we should also pay attention to the fact that from a commercial perspective, the most notable members of the "Seo Taiji right" was teenagers who had emerged as prolific consumers of popular culture. The main driving forces and agents in first-generation pop group fan bases that emerged in the mid-1990s (including acts like H.O.T) were South Koreans in their teens who had gained unquestionable purchasing power. During the 1990s, that market would fuel the establishment of the specialized music management company system exemplified by businesses such as SM, DSPmedia, and YG. This would reach its peak in the 2010s and form the foundation for South Korean popular culture's development into a global industry.

Private Broadcasting, Bodies, Contact, Lifestyles

At this point, it is important to remember the changes that were happening in the mass media environment during this period. The launch of SBS as a private commercial broadcaster in 1991 was a special event that sparked evolutions in the television era, the impact of which, was as momentous as the advent of today's countless general broadcasting channels. The arrival of private commercial broadcasting, with much of the public management aspect diluted, was a qualitative and quantitative impetus for the production of series and shows geared to audiences' consumption sensibilities. The emergence of SBS and the dissolution of exclusive contracting systems encouraged television personalities to move to different networks, stoking a viewership competition among channels. The golden age of talk shows arrived, with Choi Jinsil occupying a league of her own as a rising TV star of the 1990s. Advertising evolved along the same lines as miniseries—or rather, miniseries came to follow the advertising format. It was the full-fledged arrival of a "lifestyle" era in which TV series and commercials offered designs for living.[4]

The body transformed from an object of political control to a "product" of the kind most noted in late capitalism, emerging overtly as the central object/product in the market and advertising. Among the public, there was an explosive rise in interest in one's body as a focus of consumption. The beauty, plastic surgery, and bio-health industries had truly arrived.

Trendy series like *Jealousy* began appearing on television, and people began to covet the realities presented in such series for themselves. The lifestyle referred to Choi Jinsil's advertisements became a new guide for living, and those viewers who could not scratch those itches through consumption came to perceive their own reality as deprived. South Korea had just passed out of an era of genuine deprivation and yet here, rather than issues of wealth or poverty, happiness and unhappiness became issues of "relative deprivation" or one's ability to satisfying consumption desires. The 1990s were a true tipping point for the era of consumerism.

This trend was further accelerated by the arrival of the cable TV era in 1995 and the beginning of local private broadcasting. "Fashion," "car," "apartment," "profession," "middle class," "Gangnam," "credit card," "land," "stocks," "investment"—by the mid-to-late 1990s, these were the symbols that people most often talked about. Having barely withstood the 1980s in order to make the transition into the 1990s, people in South Korea were not becoming "citizens" as political actors; they were turning into agents of consumption. This contrasted many Western countries that went first transitioned into a civil society before shifting into a late-stage capitalism. South Korea on the other hand, in the wake of the "masses" discourse of '70s and '80s, seemed to be preparing to skip over "citizenship" and transition straight into a "consuming public." *Romantic Love and Society* (2002), a fiction collection by Jeong Yihyun, was a sort of urban anthropological report showing how the agents of 1990s lifestyles had come to shape the "body." The first-person protagonist of the story takes care of her body in order to acquire a New Beetle, Louis Vuitton fashion, and a Chanel bag; she is a subject of exchange and does not view "purity" as a moral issue. Instead, she treats it as a product or marketing strategy. This same landscape was encapsulated at the very start of the 1990s by the poet Yoo Ha, who wrote, "A street scattered with the flavor of apple, the flavor of cherry, all sorts of shoddy flavors, the scent of Wellaform mousse spray/Wendy's girls, boutique women, *dajji* [sex workers whose customers were predominantly Japanese] with Gucci bags stepping out the doors of the café high society." During the 1980s, people had hoped that in the 1990s,

4. More details on this phenomenon can be found in Kang Joonman's book cited above.

they would not only escape from poverty but also be able to meet the needs for a happy life and live in harmony with their neighbors in a more equal and democratic society. But somewhere along the way, people of the 1990s ended up surrounded by signifiers of desire. Here, happiness became an issue of relative deprivation, and a sense of discontentment only seemed to grow amid a consciousness of comparison based on material standards. The *World Happiness Report* published in 2023 by the Sustainable Development Solutions Network, a UN global initiative, ranked South Korea 57th in terms of its happiness index, placing it in the lowest tier among OECD members. We must conclude, however, that the first signs of this "indicator irony"—an inversely proportional relationship between material growth and life satisfaction—were already present in South Korea in the 1990s.

Before the 1990s, South Koreans dedicated themselves to history, believing that by changing the powers that be, they could achieve a historic transformation in the world; at the very least, they harbored these beliefs fervently in their hearts. But what drew a clear dividing line between the 1990s and the world before was not any political issue—it was the unexpected emergence of "cool" new media. In that respect, director Chang Yoonhyun's box office hit *The Contact* (1997) offered a condensed portrait of the new landscape of "modern romance" in the 1990s. Anonymously conversing through their computers, a man and woman who both nurse romantic scars go through a process of self-reconciliation and eventual actual "contact." The film offers a striking picture of communication methods used in a new media era where it was possible to meet without ever seeing another's face. Computer-based communication would go beyond the level of mere conversations online to form the distinctive public discourse environment known as "online communication culture." Bulletin boards like Chollian, Hitel, and Unitel provided settings for a new discourse culture where people could form taste-based communities or express and debate about their different social and cultural views. At the time, there were no settings in society where members of the general public and citizenry could widely share their opinions, perspectives, reviews, or commentary. The only "public discourse spheres" to speak of were the newspapers and magazines, where voices were permitted to members of socially recognized highbrow classes and expert groups. In that sense, this development signified the emergence of a historic environment for opening up pluralism of perspectives and democracy of speech. Online communication also made it possible to circulate information across barriers of time and space. This online culture would lay the groundwork for the portal site boom of the 2000s, thanks to the Kim Daejung administration's state-level effort in 1998 to create the earliest ultra-high-speed internet network in the world.

More even than the invention of the radio or television, the arrival of the internet signified the advent of truly revolutionary media. Together with the mobile phone, it can be described as the most revolutionary incident when answering the question of how to distinguish the 1980s from the eras that came after. What was the most important factor in South Korea's rise to becoming a competitive player on the global stage a scant 20 to 30 years after the 1990s? Instead of "globalization" a word bandied around as a kind of abstract catchphrase during the Kim Youngsam administration, perhaps it lay in the crucial foundation that was laid for the "digital nation" through the quick establishment of an ultra-high-speed internet network.

A New Millennium or the End of a Century?

In spite of the end of global ideological warfare and the ascendancy of political conservatism, South Korea seemed to be undergoing quantitative and qualitative expansion with an economic boom, the expansion of popular culture industries, and explosive growth in the public's demand for consumer culture. With the declaration of the default on the national debts in 1997, the country was abruptly drawn—unprepared and irreversibly—into the currents of globalization, as if declaring a decisive farewell to the socioeconomic foundation and social ideals of the preceding era. The national bankruptcy that occurred amid the global transition from industrial to financial capitalism, and the bailout agreement reached with the IMF as a solution, bore no connections at all with the ideas of universal human rights or communitarian freedom that the South Korean democratization movement had been hungering for. Francis Fukuyama declared the victory of liberalism to be the "end of history," but the "global standard" of financial capitalism imposed and adopted by way of the IMF ended up moving in a direction of dismantling society's communitarian safety net, while erasing the ideals (if not the idea) of history.

In particular, the IMF demanded the adoption of a free competition system in the labor market, while encouraging a transition to contract-based and irregular work in many categories of labor. Instantaneously, the concept of a "lifelong workplace" in South Korean society came crumbling down. Structures of permanent employment anxiety and an "unemployment society" became cemented in place. The IMF also pushed forward heavy demands for the privatization of society's public goods and services, including electricity, gas, water, railways, and healthcare. The Kim Daejung administration declared South Korea free from the IMF bailout regime after less than four years, crediting this to the public "sharing the pain." But the South Korea that followed was forever changed. The transition toward globalization imposed by the IMF had completely altered and laid waste to the mood and communitarian feelings in South Korean society.

The 1990s was a time of different forms of prosperity, when material wealth quantitatively increased and popular culture expanded to industrially significant scales. However these developments also proceeded in a direction that sheared away any communitarian prospects and sense of solidarity. The survival-centered mentality of today's South Korean individuals and the "everyone for themselves" tactics they have adopted can be seen as products of the globalization regime transplanted in the late 1990s under the IMF system. In a world that lacks ideals of unity, individuals were left with no direction, no methods, no drive to move forward. They were each consigned to their own island, trapped in their own cell, having lost sight of "history" and the "square" as a public forum. Many felt (and still feel) as if they had been cast into a jungle. Amid this sense of isolation, anxiety, and emptiness, a fin de siècle crept into the cracks. For better or worse, there was no "millennium bug" and no rapture when the clock struck midnight and 2000 arrived.

Over two decades later, it seems as though the same late-century fears are making a comeback, mutating and proliferating into different sorts of social phenomena. As we observe South Korea's spiritual and popular culture from the vantage point of 2023, one of the most noticeable things we see is the "consumption" of pseudo-religions, which has been spreading at a fast pace. Examples of these include the "new" Christian sects. Growing at an exponential rate, they seem poised to replace of traditional denominations. We see an explosive rise in Buddhism too—not the traditional forms as practiced in central and south Asia, but a watered down version, influenced by the West. We see a proliferation of various new and pseudo-religious, personal faiths, and spirituality industries. This trend is a global phenomenon as human civilization finds itself facing a serious crisis. In South Korea's case, it seems to be spreading faster, and more deeply and widely. Perhaps it is the anxious growth of the psychological seeds planted during the millennium complex of the 1990s, which emerged from the communitarian wasteland experienced in the wake of the Asian financial crisis. If that is the case, then contemporary practitioners (consumers) of meditation who focus on their breath and on "the present movement," may have detected the nature of the here and now. They understand the fact that our century may not be the beginning of a new millennium, but the beginning of the end. One "digital meditator" predicted the century to come as she observed the 1990s and shared the following prophetic words:

> *"I have had a web browser installed in my body. Bit by bit, the moon digs inside of me. God has come to live in my body. God is now a presence I can grow within my body."*

> *"At 1 p.m. on May 11, 2000, a fellow tribe member "s" and I meet at the entrance of a large shopping mall that sells nomadic items / As we prepared to relocate to our winter ground, "s" and I require the herding and nomadic supplies of the gods."*[5]

5. Yi Won, *A Thousand Moons Float in the River Yahoo!* (Seoul: Moonji, 2001).

Hahm Donkyoon is a literary and civilization critic, as well as a learning designer. He has taught literature, philosophy, and art theory at renowned universities such as Korea University, Ewha Womans University, and Korea National University of Arts. In addition, he has designed and consulted on innovative humanities and arts education programs for multiple institutions including the Ministry of Culture, Sports, and Tourism, Seoul Open City University, Seoul Foundation for Arts and Culture, Samsung Electronics, Leeum Museum of Art, Foundation Academia Platonica, and municipal offices of education. Throughout the course of his career, Hahm has worked as director of the Humanities Lab at Paju Typography Institute, HK Research Professor at the Research Institute of Korean Studies at Korea University, director of Citizen Planet, and founding editor-in-chief for Hyundai Motor's heritage book project. Currently, he is the owner of Sitabookbar, an independent bookstore located in Jeju, and the CEO of Urban Spiritual Company dasding. Furthermore, he holds a visiting professorship at Myongji University's Department of Creative Writing. Hahm is a prolific author with over 10 published books to his name—notable titles among them are *Philosophy of The Thing* and *Philosophy of The Moment*.

A New Era of Division, and Paradigm Shift in Art

Art from the 1990s and 2000s reflected the monumental changes in the global constitution as well as related developments in Korea's social environment. Contemporary Korean art from this period was both universal and specific and is only properly understood by taking the global dimension and internal contexts unique to Korea into account. "Contemporaneity" enables a deviation from the system that addresses or perceives situations and states in terms of sequential and linear flows of time and space; it relates to valuation that reflect times, places, situations, and conditions that are complex and entangled. By considering the artistic practices of the time, the exhibition attempts to identify which contexts made such perspectives possible.

1990년대를 관통하여 2000년대로 이어지는 이 시기의 미술은 마치 지각 변동과도 같은 전 세계적 체질 변화 상황과 이와 연관된 한국의 사회 환경을 그대로 흡수했다. 그래서 동시대 한국 현대미술은 보편적이면서 특정적이고, 전 세계적인 차원과 우리 사회 내적 맥락을 함께 고려할 때 제대로 이해할 수 있다. '동시대성'은 상황과 사태를 순차적이고 선형적인 시공간의 흐름으로 다루거나 인식하는 체계와는 다른 접근을 가능하게 하는 것으로, 복합적이고 뒤얽힌 시공간과 상황, 조건들을 수용하는 판단 가치와 관련되어 있다. 이와 같은 관점의 바탕이 되는 맥락을 당대 발현된 미술 행위들에서 확인하고자 한다.

시대 변환과 미술 지형 변동

공성훈

KONG Sunghun

공성훈(1965–2021)은 서울대학교에서 서양화를, 서울산업대학교에서 전자공학을 전공했다. 이후 서울대학교 대학원 서양화과를 졸업했다. 작가는 1990년대 예술과 비예술에 대해 질문을 던지고 다양한 매체를 실험했다. 1990년대 ≪로고스와 파토스≫(1993), ≪뼈≫(1995), ≪싹≫(1995) 등 전시에서 개념적인 설치작업을 선보였는데, 2000년대 초부터는 다시 본격 회화를 통해 익숙한 일상을 소재로 한 풍경화에 집중했다. 2013년 MMCA 올해의 작가상 수상자로 선정되며 '심리적 차원에서 밀도 높은' 회화를 보여주는 작가로 평가받았다.

Kong Sunghun (1965–2021) majored in Western painting at Seoul National University and studied electronic engineering at the Seoul National University of Technology (now the SEOULTECH) before earning a graduate degree in Western painting from SNU. During the 1990s, he embarked on an experimental artistic career in which he used his conceptual installation and multi-slide projection work to raise questions about commercialized art and the art/non-art distinction and to criticize the Korean art education system. Kong took part in several contemporary experimental exhibitions, including *Logos and Pathos* (1993), *Bone* (1995), and *Sprout* (1995). In the late 1990s, and Kong shifted toward the traditional medium of painting, producing landscape images that captured everyday scenes from 2000. He won the MMCA's Korea Artists Prize in 2013 and was evaluated as an artist who reveals the human psychological dimension.

〈블라인드 작업〉은 블라인드를 활용하여 작업한 공성훈의 초기 연작 중 하나로, 전기모터가 장착된 4개의 블라인드를 '엑스(X)자' 형태로 설치한 작품이다. 작가는 블라인드 날개를 순차적으로 형광 페인트로 칠하고, 그 뒷면에는 알루미늄 테이프를 붙였다. 모터를 작동하면 블라인드가 천천히 열렸다 닫혔다 하면서 빛을 반사한다. 일상적 사물인 블라인드는 본래의 기능을 잃은 채, 색채, 형태, 그리고 움직임 등 시지각적 요소로서 제시된다. 작가는 대량 생산된 소재를 단순한 제작방식을 통해 그 의미를 최소화하면서 매체 실험에 집중했다. 보편적 개념이나 가치보다는 "구체적인 것"에서 미술을 다시 시작하고 싶다는 생각으로 전자공학을 공부했던 작가의 초기 작업 태도를 반영하는 작품이다.

Blind-Work (1992) is part of an early series by Kong Sunghun that makes use of blinds. Four sets of blinds, each with an attached electric motor, have been installed in the shape of an "X". The artist has progressively applied fluorescent paint in a spectral design along the blades of the blinds, with aluminum tape affixed to the rear surface. The work is designed to reflect light in space through the repeated slow opening and closing of the blinds as the attached motors operate. The blinds have shed its original role and are presented in terms of its visual and other perceptual elements, including color, shape, and movement. With his use of mass-produced materials and limited, simple creation methods, Kong minimizes the "significance" of his work and focuses more on experimenting with media. The work reflects the early approach of the artist, who studied electrical engineering out of a desire to ground his art in "concrete things" rather than universal concepts or values.

블라인드 작업
Blind-Work

1992

국립현대미술관 소장
MMCA collection

블라인드 4개, 페인트, 알루미늄 테이프, 모터
Four blind curtains, paint, aluminium tape, motor

100×100cm(×4)

〈버추얼 버추얼 리얼리티〉(1994)는 1994년 대전 엑스포과학공원 개관 기념전인 《기술과 정보 그리고 환경의 미술》 출품 작품이다. 작가는 만화경과 헬멧을 이용한 기계 장치를 선보였다. 매우 단순한 기술과 장치를 활용한 이 작품의 제목은 역설적으로 첨단 과학기술이 적용된 가상현실(VR) 기기를 연상하게 한다. 이를 통해 작가는 고도의 과학 기술에 대한 자신의 복잡다단한 시각을 담아내면서 '실재와 가상'이라는 오랜 화두를 건드리고 있다.

Virtual Virtual Reality (1994) was presented at Technology, Information, and Environment Art, a commemorative exhibition for the opening of the Daejeon Expo Park in 1994. Kong Sunghun presented a crude mechanical device that combined a helmet with a kaleidoscope designed to be powered by a motor. As the title suggests, this work ironically uses simple technology to evoke associations with virtual reality devices that rely on advanced science and technology. The artist is expressing a critical perspective on science and technology, while also recalling the age-old artistic themes of "reality" and "imagination."

버추얼 버추얼 리얼리티
Virtual Virtual Reality

1994

국립현대미술관 소장
MMCA collection

헬멧, 거울, 모터, 플렉시글라스
Helmet, mirror, motor, plexiglass

57×28×56cm

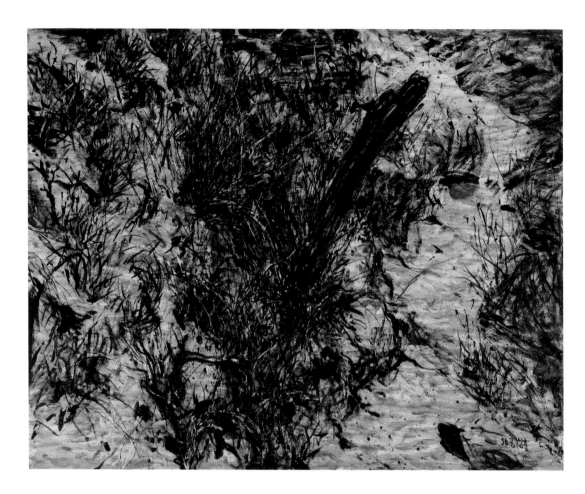

먼지 그림 (뒷산에서)
Dust Painting (at Mountain)

1996

국립현대미술관 소장
MMCA collection

캔버스에 먼지, 아크릴릭 물감
Dust and acrylic paint on canvas

181.8×227.3cm

〈먼지 그림 (뒷산에서)〉(1996)은 접착제를 섞은 먼지와 아크릴릭 물감을 사용하여 마을 뒷산에서 본 풍경을 담은 회화 연작 '먼지 그림' 중 하나다. 붓의 자유분방한 움직임으로 채워진 화면은 언뜻 보면 마치 추상화와 같은 인상을 주지만, 가까이 다가가서 자세히 들여다보면 회화 표면은 지저분한 먼지로 가득하다. 작가는 종종 먼지를 자기 신체의 일부이자 "분신"에 빗대어 언급한 바 있는데, 이 연작 이후 작가는 작업의 초점을 외부로부터 자기 자신에게로 이동시키고 '몸'을 소재로 한 멀티슬라이드 프로젝션 연작을 발표하기도 했다.

Dust Painting (at Mountain) (1996) is one of artist Kong Sunghun's series of Dust Paintings, in which he used acrylic paints and dust mixed with adhesive to capture a landscape seen around a mountain in back of a village. Filled with free-form brushstrokes, the canvas resembles a work of Abstract Expressionism when seen from a distance, but on closer inspection, the viewer can see that the image has been formed from dust. He also emphasized an autobiographical aspect by likening the dust to a part of his own body or an alter ego. Afterward, he would shift the focus of his work from the external world to himself, presenting his multi-slide projection series of works centering on the body.

개
A Dog

2001

국립현대미술관 소장
MMCA collection

112.3×145cm

캔버스에 유화 물감
Oil paint on canvas

공성훈은 1990년대 후반 경기도 고양시 벽제동으로 이사하면서 동네 주변에서 목격한 일상 풍경을 화폭에 옮기며 ⟨벽제의 밤⟩ 연작을 시작했다. 늦은 밤 집으로 돌아오는 길에 작가가 마주한 장면은 낮과는 전혀 다른 모습을 드러내 보이는 풍경이었다. ⟨개⟩(2001)는 ⟨벽제의 밤⟩ 연작 중 하나로, 개 한 마리가 어슬렁거리며 돌아다니고 있는 어두운 밤 풍경을 보여준다. 마치 조명을 강하게 받은 듯이 붉게 빛나는 화면 중앙은 짙은 색조의 주변 분위기에 싸여 시각적 대조를 이룬다. 배회하는 개의 움직임이 포착된 장면으로, 개의 형체가 어렴풋하게 드러나는 까닭에 화면에는 알 수 없는 긴장감이 느껴진다.

In the late 1990s, Kong Sunghun moved to the neighborhood of Byeokje in Goyang, a city in Gyeonggi-do, and began producing his *A Night at Byeokje* series, in which he transferred the everyday scenes he saw around him onto the canvas. The images he encountered on his way home after work late at night represented a dual landscape that appeared different from how it looked during the day. *A Dog* (2001) is part of the *A Night at Byeokje* series, showing a dark nightscape where a lone dog can be seen wandering. The canvas seems to glow red, while the center creates a striking contrast as it appears ringed by the black night air. The painting is both fascinating and artificial, achieved by the depth of color produced with adept brushstrokes and the exaggerated sheen of the surface. The feelings of anxiety and tension are heightened by the blurred depiction of figure making it difficult to discern concrete shapes.

〈개〉(2001)는 〈벽제의 밤〉 연작 중 하나로, 화면 전체에
푸른빛이 감도는 어둠 속, 목줄이 매인 개 한 마리가
등장하는 작품이다. 마치 카메라 플래시가 터진 듯한 광경을
보여주는 이 작품 속 개는 인간의 감춰진 욕망과 두려움을
의미하는 듯하다. 깊은 어둠 안에서 정면을 응시하고
있는 개의 눈동자는 마주하고 있으나 보이지 않는 존재를
암시하며 불안한 분위기를 자아낸다.

This work titled *A Dog* (2001) is part of the *A Night at
Byeokje* series, showing a dog on a leash in a dark
setting with swirls of blue. With the coarse application
of white paint, the canvas depicts a scene as if it were
captured in the moment by a camera's flash. The dogs
that often appear in Kong's work from this period
seem to symbolize the hidden instincts, desires, and
fears of human beings. As the dog stares forward
through the darkness, its eyes hint at an unseen
presence, evoking in the viewer an unsettling feeling.

개
A Dog

2001

국립현대미술관 소장
MMCA collection

130×162.2cm

캔버스에 유화 물감
Oil paint on canvas

모텔
Motel

2007

국립현대미술관 소장
MMCA collection

캔버스에 아크릴릭 물감
Acrylic paint on canvas

130.5×193.5cm

〈모텔〉(2007)은 작가가 출퇴근하며 늘 지나다니는 길에 줄지어 늘어선 모텔들의 밤 풍경을 담고 있는 작품이다. 마치 서구의 고전적 건축과도 같은 건물, 화려한 조명, 자극적인 문구의 네온사인 광고판 등은 화면 곳곳에서 불편함과 불안함, 그리고 키치적 감성을 드러낸다. 그림 중앙 상단에는 어두운 밤 붉은 가로등이 켜진 공원의 모습이 보인다. 근경과 원경이 재구성된 이 풍경은 실재를 그대로 재현한 것이 아니다. 작가는 서로 다른 장소에서 촬영한 사진 이미지들을 재조합하여 또 다른 풍경을 직조해 놓았다.

Motel (2007) presents a nightscape on the outskirts of the city with rows of motels. The image evokes a sense of kitsch with a building in the shape of a medieval castle, neon signs relaying provocative advertisements, and various other brightly colored lights. Visible in the darkness of the night sky above is a portion of landscape showing a park lit with red street lights. The break with perspective in the canvas composition indicates that the landscape depicted is not a faithful representation of a real scene. The artist has contributed an unreal quality by combining photographs taken in different locations to form a single image.

박이소

BAHC Yiso

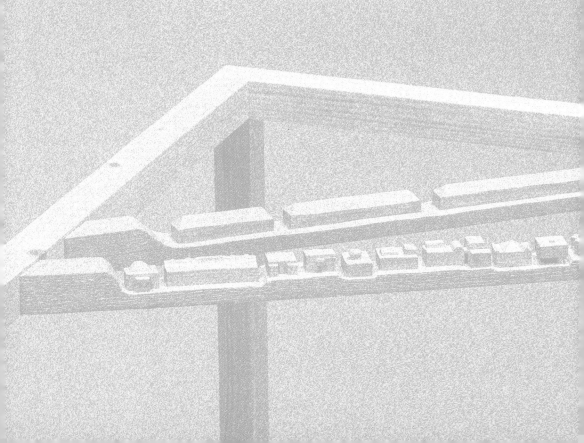

박이소(1957–2004)는 1980년대 중반 이후 2000년대 초까지 뉴욕과 서울을 배경으로 다양한 활동을 전개해 온 작가이다. 그는 예술가, 미술 공간 운영자, 기획자, 평론가, 교육자 등 시각예술을 토대로 소통과 문화번역의 문제를 끊임없이 고민하고 실천한 인물이다. 뉴욕에서 대학원을 졸업한 1985년부터 서울의 삼성디자인교육원(SADI) 교수로 근무하게 되어 귀국한 1995년까지 약 10년간을 '뉴욕 시기', 이후 한국을 기반으로 활동했던 2004년까지 시기를 '서울 시기'로 구분한다. 귀국 후에는 기존의 가명 '박모' 대신 '박이소'라는 이름으로 활동하며 이전과는 또 다르게 차별적인 작업과 활동을 열정적으로 전개했다. 1997년 광주비엔날레, 2001년 요코하마트리엔날레 등 다수의 국제 비엔날레 등 해외 미술행사에 초대되었다. 2002년에는 에르메스재단 미술상을 받고 2003년에는 베니스비엔날레 한국관 작가로 선정되는 등 활발하게 활동을 이어갔으나 2004년 갑작스레 심장마비로 사망했다. 사후 2006년 로댕갤러리, 2014년 아트선재센터, 그리고 2018년 국립현대미술관에서 회고전이 열렸다.

Bahc Yiso (1957–2004) was a New York—and Seoul—based artist who engaged in various artistic practices over a career spanning from the mid-1980s to his untimely death in 2004. As an artist, art space operator, curator, critic, and educator, he adopted visual arts as the foundation of his practice while endlessly contemplating questions of communication and his relationship with the society that surrounded him. His "New York period" lasted for around a decade between his completion of graduate studies in New York in 1985 and his return to Korea in 1995 as a professor at the Samsung Art and Design Institute (SADI) in Seoul. His "Seoul period," followed, as he continued to live in Korea until his death in 2004. After returning to Korea, he worked under the name "Bahc Yiso" instead of his previous artistic name, "Bahc Mo." All activities he undertook during this time were both passionate and distinct from those prior. He was invited to numerous international biennials and other overseas art events, including the Gwangju Biennale in 1997 and the Yokohama Triennale in 2001. He was awarded the Hermès Foundation Missulsang in 2002 and selected as an artist for the Korean Pavilion of the 2003 Venice Biennale. Sadly, his prolific activity came to an abrupt end when he suffered a fatal heart attack in 2004. Since his death, his retrospective exhibitions have been held at Rodin Gallery in 2006, Art Sonje Center in 2014, and the MMCA in 2018.

〈역사의 문/역사적인 문〉(1987) 화면 가장자리에는 문(門)이라는 한자가 거꾸로 자리하고 있어 마치 옛 전통 가옥의 문처럼 위치해 있고 그 중앙에는 토끼가 있다. 원래 캔버스 상단에 검은 색 플라스틱 솥이 붙어 있었는데 현재는 유실되었다. 1987–1989년 작가 작업 노트에는 '과학적', '비과학적', '정치적', '비정치적', '전통적', '비전통적', '감정적', '양심적', '상징적' 등 '–적'이라는 단어가 자주 등장한다. 이와 같은 형용사는 받아들이는 사람에 따라 그 정도의 차이가 있기 때문에 의미는 끊임없이 차이를 생산한다. '역사'가 '역사적'이라는 형용사로 변할 때 다양한 해석이 가능해지고 의미 역시 덧붙여진다. 화면 속 토끼 이미지는 박이소의 스케치와 작품에서 자주 등장하는 모티프이다. 토끼 형상의 의미에 대해 일견 한국적 감수성의 '달토끼'라고 읽어내는 이도 있고, 한반도를 의미한다는 해석도 있지만 정작 박이소는 그 의미를 정확히 밝힌 바 없다.

On the edge of the canvas, there are the Chinese character meaning "gate" or "entrance" (門) has been inverted in a position resembling gate of a traditional Korean house, and a rabbit in the center. A black plastic rice cooker was hanged over this, although it has since been lost. The artist's notes between 1987 and 1989 include many adjectives, such as "scientific/non-scientific," "emotional," "conscientious," "symbolic," "political/non-political," and "traditional/ non-traditional." Unlike nouns, which have fixed meanings, adjectives may be perceived as having different states and degrees by different individuals. Their meaning is fluid, rather than remaining fixed as any one thing. When the word "history" is transformed into the adjective "historic(al)," this allows for various external readings, while also opening up the possibility for appropriation of its meaning. The rabbit that appears in the work also appears in many other idea sketches and artworks by Bahc Yiso. Some see it as signifying the similarly rabbit-shaped Korean Peninsula, while others interpret it as a reflection of the Korean sensibilities represented by the "rabbit in the moon." Bahc himself never said exactly what it meant.

역사의 문/역사적인 문
Entrance of History

1987

국립현대미술관 소장
MMCA collection

캔버스에 아크릴릭 물감
Acrylic paint on canvas

181.4×187cm

〈삼위일체〉(1994)는 작가의 뉴욕 시기 후반에 제작된 주요 작품 중 하나다. 커피, 콜라, 간장으로 각기 세 개의 별을 그려 넣은 〈쓰리 스타 쇼〉(1994)에 이어 이 3가지 액체를 섞어 국수 한 그릇으로 그려 놓았다. 〈삼위일체〉는 〈호모 아이덴트로푸스〉(1994) 등과 함께 뉴욕 시기 작가의 심도 있는 탐구의 주제였던 '정체성'이라는 주제의 마무리를 담아내고 있다. 야구방망이를 간장에 절인 〈무제〉(1994)와 마찬가지로 이 작품 또한 문화적 상호침투의 가능성 여부를 다루고 있다. 작가는 단색으로 단순하게 그림으로써 각 용액들이 연관되어 있는 사회문화적 맥락에 관한 정보는 제공하고 있지 않다. 결국 '정체성'이라는 문제를 사회문화적 패권과 연결하기보다는 오히려 인간의 내재적 조건과 관계하는 것임을 보여주고자 했다.

One of the most prominent works produced in the later period of Bahc Yiso's time in New York, *Trinity* (1994) forms a pairing of sorts with his *Three Star Show* (1994). In that work, he painted three stars using coffee, cola, and soy sauce for each; here, he mixes all three together to paint a single bowl of noodles. Alongside the work *Homo Identropous* (1994), which was produced around the same time, it symbolically illustrates the end of his long explorations of the theme of "identity" while he was in New York. Much like Bahc's *Untitled* (1994), in which he soaked an American baseball bat in soy sauce, this work alludes strongly to both the potential for and impossibility of mutual cultural permeation. By omitting all contextual information besides the neutral outward form of the work, the artist conceals its actual meaning from the viewer. He is deliberately erasing the labels of cultural identity that inevitably follow individual objects around.

삼위일체
Trinity

1994

국립현대미술관 소장
MMCA collection

종이에 커피, 콜라, 간장을 섞은 용액
Mixed solution with coffee, cola and soy sauce
on paper

131×101cm

〈무제〉(1994)는 〈삼위일체〉와 마찬가지로 박이소의 뉴욕 시기 후반에 제작된 작품 중 하나이다. 작가는 미국을 야구방망이로, 한국을 간장으로 비유하여 간장에 야구방망이를 절여 놓음으로써 사회문화적 소통 또는 상호침투의 가능성과 불가능성을 다루었다. 소통과 상호이해가 진정 가능한지 불가능한지를 끊임없이 탐구했다. 작품을 보면 아크릴로 된 원통은 마개로 완벽하게 밀봉하여 간장 냄새를 완벽하게 차단하고자 했고, 야구방망이의 경우, 손잡이 부분만 겨우 보이게 함으로써 각각의 해당 사물이 암시하는 사회문화적 정체성의 의미를 의도적으로 지워버리고 있다.

Untitled (1994) is one of the representative works produced by Bahc Yiso during the later portion of his time in New York. With the baseball bat (representing America) soaking in soy sauce (representing Korea), this work alludes strongly to both the potential for and impossibility of mutual cultural permeation. He constantly explored whether communication and mutual understanding were entirely possible or impossible. By sealing off the acrylic tube completely with a stopper to block the smell of soy sauce and by setting the bat up in such a way that only part of its handle appears, he is deliberately erasing the labels of cultural identity that inevitably follow the individual objects around. Through this, he visually represents the idea that the tasks associated with "identity" are not imposed by cultural or power-based dominance, but rather are instilled as an internal condition within people.

무제
Untitled

1994

국립현대미술관 소장
MMCA collection

112×61×21cm

나무, 아크릴 튜브, 간장, 야구방망이, 합성수지
Wood, acrylic tube, soy sauce, baseball bat, synthetic resin

〈베니스 비엔날레〉(2003)와 함께 2003년 제50회 베니스비엔날레 한국관에 전시된 〈2010년 세계에서 가장 높은 건축물 1위–10위〉(2003)는 작가가 직접 7년 후인 2010년 세계에서 가장 높을 건축물 1위부터 10위를 조사하고 이를 근거로 그 모형을 백색 유토로 제작한 작품이다. 작가는 무릎 높이 정도의 낮은 좌대에 모형들을 줄지어 배치함으로써 그 크기를 비교할 수 있게 했다. 2위–10위까지를 대략 70cm 정도 높이로 비슷하게 만들었고, 가장 높은 건물은 130cm 높이의 원통형 PVC 파이프로 제작했다. 작가는 견고하지 않고 물렁물렁하며 값싼 재료를 사용해 세계 유수의 고층 건축물들을 일부러 엉성하게 제작함으로써 실제 이들 건축에 투영되어 있는 인간의 욕망, 그 허무함을 다루고 있다.

For his work *World's Top Ten Tallest Structures in 2010* (2003), which was presented at the Korean Pavilion of the 50th Venice Biennale in 2003, Bahc Yiso researched and envisioned the ten tallest structures as of the year 2010. He then produced small versions in white plasticine and arranged them on a low pedestal. The structures are placed on low pedestals to allow a comparison of their actual sizes. The work includes reproductions of the second—to tenth—ranked structures at a scale of around 70cm, while the world's tallest structure has been reproduced at a larger scale of 130cm, using cylindrical PVC pipes. With his approach of deliberate crudeness through the use of flimsy, inexpensive materials, Bahc is caricaturing the various elements projected onto high-rise structures— the human feelings of desire and emptiness.

2010년 세계에서 가장 높은
건축물 1위–10위
World's Top Ten Tallest
Structures in 2010

2003/2018, 2023

국립현대미술관 소장
MMCA collection

유토, 파이프, 알루미늄 좌대
Plastiline, pipe, aluminum table

130×180×80cm

작가가 남긴 드로잉 그리고 《박이소: 기록과 기억》(2018.7.26.–12.16., MMCA 과천) 설치를 바탕으로 재구성
Reconstructed based on the artist's drawings and the installation *Bahc Yiso; Memos and Memories*
(July 26–December 16, 2018, MMCA Gwacheon)

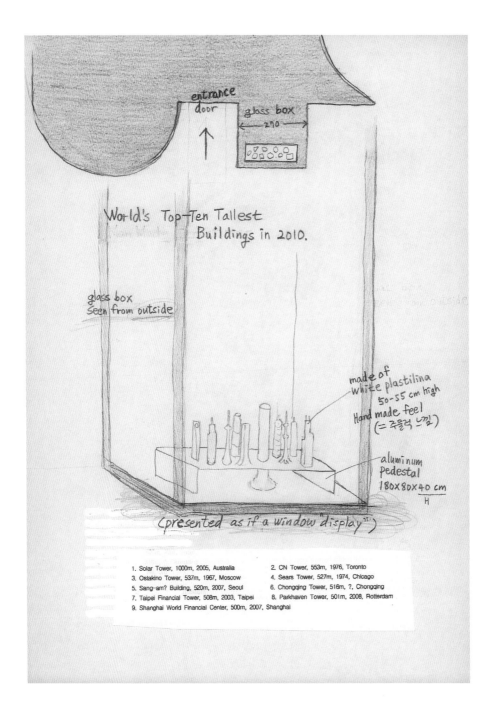

⟨2010년 세계에서 가장 높은
건축물 1위–10위⟩를 위한 드로잉
Drawing for *World's Top Ten
Tallest Structures in 2010*

2003

국립현대미술관 미술연구센터 소장,
이소사랑방 기증
MMCA Art Research Center Collection,
Gift of Yiso Sarangbang

종이에 연필, 색연필
Pencil, colored pencil
on paper

29.7×21cm

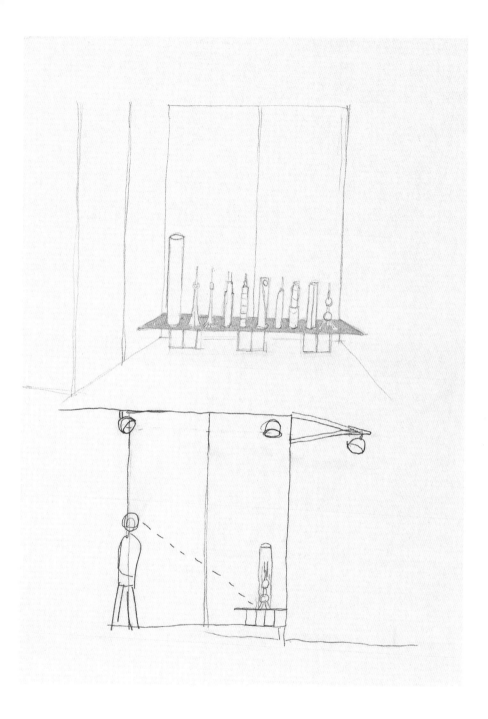

⟨2010년 세계에서 가장 높은
건축물 1위–10위⟩를 위한 드로잉
**Drawing for *World's Top Ten
Tallest Structures in 2010***

2003

국립현대미술관 미술연구센터 소장,
이소사랑방 기증
MMCA Art Research Center Collection,
Gift of Yiso Sarangbang

종이에 연필, 마커
Pencil, marker on paper

29.7×21cm

베니스 비엔날레
Venice Biennale

2003/2023

국립현대미술관 소장
MMCA collection

각목, 대야, 물, 타일, 자갈, 콘크리트
Wood, basins, water, tiles, pebbles, concrete

161×290×230cm

2003년 제50회 베니스비엔날레 한국관 작가로 선정된 박이소는 각목으로 제작한 위태로운 구조물 〈베니스 비엔날레〉를 한국관 건물 앞마당에 설치했다. 직사각형 구조의 각목은 물을 채운 4개의 세숫대야에 각각 수직의 각목으로 다리를 내려 버티고 있다. 대야의 물은 베니스 섬 주변 바다를 의미하고, 각목의 사각 틀은 세계적인 미술 행사인 비엔날레를 개최하는 베니스 시를 상징한다. 사각의 각목 프레임 모서리에 사선으로 걸쳐진 2개의 각목에는 각각 자르디니공원에 있는 26개의 국가관, 그리고 3개의 아르세날레 주제관이 약 3cm 크기의 조각으로 나란히 배치되어 있다. 국가관들의 실제 규모와 크기가 각기 다르지만 작가의 작품 속 미니어처 조각에서는 유사한 크기로 동일화되어 있다. 박이소는 이를 통해 작가 자신의 욕망 표출 창구이자 동시에 문화 패권주의의 표상인 비엔날레 국가관과 비엔날레의 권위에 물음을 던졌다.

After being selected as an artist at the Korean Pavilion for the 2003 Venice Biennale, Bahc Yiso placed a flimsy and crudely constructed wooden structure on the lawn in front of the pavilion. The four timber rods form a square framework, their legs dangling down into four different basins filled with water. The water in the basins symbolizes the sea bordering Venice, while the square framework represents the city hosting the biennale. Two timber rods are placed diagonally over the corner of the frame, with the 26 national pavilions at the Giardini della Biennale carved at a scale of roughly three centimeters. They are positioned side-by-side with the three Arsenale pavilions. While the actual pavilions differed in size and dimensions, they have been presented here at similar scales. Bahc reduces and simplifies the pavilions as channels for expressing desires and symbols of cultural hegemony, thereby questioning and lampooning the biennial's authority.

작품 일부 소실로 인해 작가 드로잉 및 기록을 근거로 재구성
Reconstructed based on the artist's drawings and records due to partial loss of the artwork

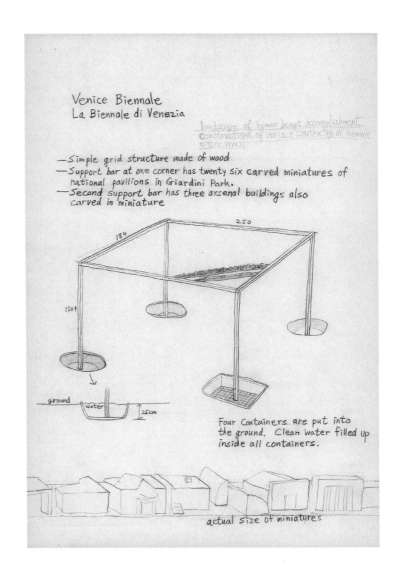

Venice Biennale
La Biennale di Venezia

landscape of human being's accomplishment
construction of Venice + construction of biennale
토포리 거지기

—Simple grid structure made of wood
—Support bar at one corner has twenty six carved miniatures of
  national pavilions in Giardini Park.
—Second support bar has three arsenal buildings also
  carved in miniature

250
184
150+
ground water 25cm

Four Containers are put into
the ground. Clean water filled up
inside all containers.

actual size of miniatures

〈베니스 비엔날레〉를 위한 드로잉
Drawing for *Venice Biennale*

2003

국립현대미술관 미술연구센터 소장,
이소사랑방 기증
MMCA Art Research Center Collection,
Gift of Yiso Sarangbang

종이에 연필, 색연필
Pencil, colored pencil on paper

29.7×21cm

베니스 비엔날레
Venice Biennale

2003

국립현대미술관 미술연구센터 소장,
이소사랑방 기증
MMCA Art Research Center Collection,
Gift of Yiso Sarangbang

〈베니스 비엔날레〉 전시전경
Installation view of *Venice Biennale*

김범

KIM Beom

김범(1963–)은 서울대학교 미술대학과 동 대학원을 졸업한 뒤 미국 뉴욕의 스쿨 오브 비주얼 아트 대학원을 졸업했다. 작가는 일상 속 평범한 사물과 상황을 유머러스하게 뒤집어 우리의 지각이 익숙하게 여겼던 현상에 또 다른 의미를 부여하는 방식으로 작업한다. 회화, 조각, 비디오, 드로잉, 출판물, 설치 등 다양한 매체와 방법론을 가지고 창작활동을 해오고 있다. 김범은 사물의 기능과 형태, 그리고 이를 지칭하는 언어 사이의 관계를 바탕으로 기존 질서와 체계에 대한 고정관념을 비트는 데 관심을 가졌다. 광주비엔날레(1997, 2002, 2012), 이스탄불비엔날레(2003), 베니스비엔날레(2005), 미디어시티서울(2010), 샤르쟈비엔날레(2015) 등에 초대받았으며, 석남미술상(1995), 에르메스 미술상(2001)을 받았다.

Kim Beom (b. 1963) completed his undergraduate and graduate studies at the Seoul National University College of Fine Arts before finishing a graduate degree at the School of Visual Arts in the United States. His artistic approach typically involves humorously inverting familiar objects and situations, as he applies utterly new meanings to things we view as familiar or take for granted. In his artistic activities, he makes use of various media, including sculpture, video, drawing, and publishing. Focusing on the relationships among objects' functions and shapes and the language used to denote them, he has shown an interest in disrupting or transforming established orders. Kim has taken part in the Gwangju Biennale (1997, 2002, 2012), the Istanbul Biennial (2003), the Venice Biennale (2005), Media City Seoul (2010), and the Sharjah Biennial (2015). He was awarded the Seoknam Art Award (1995) and the Hermès Foundation Missulsang (2001).

〈무제 (닭 요리하기)〉(1991)는 김범이 실재 대상과 이미지의 인지적 상관관계를 탐구하던 시기에 텔레비전에서 방송된 요리 프로그램을 보고 제작한 작품 중 하나이다. 작가는 요리 프로그램을 진행하는 미국의 유명 요리사 줄리아 차일드(Julia Child) 음성의 지시대로 '닭 그림'을 요리하는 모습을 영상으로 연출했다. 실제 닭 대신 종이에 그려진 닭 이미지를 마치 진짜 닭인양 정성스레 손질한 다음 오일을 바르고 접시에 담아내는 과정 후 마무리 멘트와 함께 마치 갓 요리된 음식처럼 복사기에 출력하는 다소 우스꽝스러운 상황을 연출한다. 이 종이로 닭 요리하는 행위는 당시 작가가 고민하던 대상과 이미지 간의 비논리성을 담아내고 있다.

Untitled (Cooking Chicken) (1991) is an early work by Kim Beom that draws upon the format of a cooking program. He produced it at a time when he was creating paintings on the relationship between images and actual objects. He presents a sequence where he prepares a painting of chicken by following the spoken instructions of the famous American chef Julia Child, which can be heard on a TV program. After carefully preparing a piece of paper with a drawing of a chicken (rather than an actual chicken), he applies oil and spices; the image of the artwork emerging from a copier like a finished "dish" over the closing words of the program may elicit laughter from the viewer. This comical approach is a reflection of what the artist sees as the illogicality of the relationship between the actual object and the image of it.

무제(닭 요리하기)
Untitled (Cooking Chicken)

1991

국립현대미술관 소장
MMCA collection

단채널 영상, 컬러, 사운드
Single-channel video, color, sound

4분
4 min.

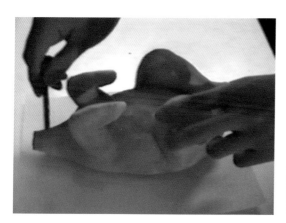

검은 테이프 위를 달리는 머리
Head Running on the Black Tape

1991

국립현대미술관 소장
MMCA collection

단채널 영상, 컬러, 사운드
Single-channel video, color, sound

2분 11초
2 min. 11 sec.

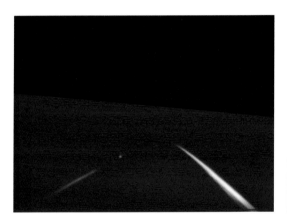

〈검은 테이프 위를 달리는 머리〉(1991)는 비디오테이프와 비디오 헤드를 가지고 도로를 달리는 차량에 빗대어 이를 통해 비디오의 구조적 특성을 드러내 보이고자 한 작품이다. 시작부터 끝나는 지점까지 어두운 2차선 도로를 달리는 영상 화면 속에서는 「그리스인 조르바」 영화의 삽입곡 「삶은 계속된다」가 흘러나온다. 이는 시간성에 초점을 맞추기 위한 장치로, 김범의 작품 중 유일하게 음악이 사용된 경우다. 작가는 당시 미발표작을 포함해서 〈버겐라인 애비뉴 서쪽 8/22/93 오후 3시〉(1993), 〈3개의 세계(에셔에 의한, 청계고가도로 1/13/97 5:00–5:20 a.m.)〉(1997), 〈꽃〉(1999) 등을 통해 시간성을 다루는 매체인 비디오에 대한 실험적 작품 제작을 수년간 지속했다.

Drawing parallels between a video tape/video head and a vehicle traveling along a highway, *Head Running on the Black Tape* (1991) is a work that attempts to depict the structural nature of video as a linear recording medium. Throughout the video, the image on screen follows along a darkened two-lane highway while the song *Life Goes On* from the film *Zorba the Greek* plays on the soundtrack. Intended as a device to emphasize linear temporality, this is the only example of music being used in Kim Beom's body of work. Around this time, Kim spent several years creating experimental pieces that examined the meaning of linear recording media, including *Bergenline Avenue West 8/22/93, 3 p.m.* (1993), *Three Worlds (After Escher, Chung Gye Skyway 1/13/97 5:00–5:20 a.m.)* (1997), and *Flower* (1999), as well as other unreleased works.

<3개의 세계(에셔에 의한, 청계고가도로 1/13/97 5:00–5:20 a.m.)>는 1997년 일본 시세이도 갤러리에서 개최되었던 《아시아의 산보》에 출품했던 작품이다. 지금은 철거되고 없는 서울 청계고가도로를 빠르게 달리는 택시의 백미러를 이용해서 촬영했다. 반대쪽에서 달려오는 차들, 택시 옆을 스치며 백미러 속으로 멀어지는 차들, 그리고 작가가 승차해 있는 차량의 백미러에 비치는 풍경들을 하나의 화면 안에 담은 것으로, 과거, 현재, 미래라는 시간의 응축과 교차, 안과 밖이라는 공간의 접합 등이 다뤄지고 있다. 이 같은 구성은 네덜란드 판화가 M. C. 에셔(M. C. Escher)가 <3개의 세계>(1995)라는 판화 작품에서 물 표면에 비친 나무와 수면 위에 떠다니는 나뭇잎, 그리고 물 아래로 헤엄치는 물고기를 하나의 화면에 담아 3개의 공간적 차원을 교차시킨 시도에서 착안했다. 김범은 고가도로라는 장소가 지닌 움직임과 속도를 통해 해당 공간의 시간적 특성을 포착하고자 했다. 그런가 하면 90도로 회전된 영상 화면을 통해 비디오테이프의 구조와 시간에 따라 변화하는 도로 위의 움직임을 물리적으로 일치시키고자 했다.

Three Worlds (After Escher, Chung Gye Skyway 1/13/97 5:00–5:20 a.m.) (1997) is a video work that was produced and presented for *Asian Walk*, a 1997 exhibition at Japan's Shiseido Gallery with artists from Korea, China, and Japan taking part. It was filmed via the rearview mirror of a taxi that runs fast on the Cheonggye Skyway in Seoul, which was demolished present. Through the traveling cars, the approaching landscape, and the spaces disappearing in the rearview mirror, he juxtaposes temporal dimensions (past, present, and future) with spatial ones (inside/outside, mirrors) on a single screen. The composition takes its motif from the three different spatial dimensions that appear in the Dutch print artist M. C. Escher's work *Three Worlds* (1995), in which a single image shows trees reflected on the surface of the water, the surface with leaves floating on it, and fish swimming underneath. In this way, Kim is trying to show the temporal characteristics of a space through the movements and speeds associated with a particular setting. By rotating the video screen 90 degrees, he can be seen attempting to physically align the movements over the highway as time passes with the structure of the videotape medium.

**3개의 세계(에셔에 의한, 청계고가도로
1/13/97 5:00–5:20 a.m.)**
*Three Worlds (After Escher, Chung Gye
Skyway 1/13/97 5:00–5:20 a.m.)*

1997

국립현대미술관 소장
MMCA collection

단채널 영상, 흑백, 무음
Single-channel video, black and white,
silent

6분 35초
6 min. 35 sec.

이동기

LEE Dongi

이동기(1967–)는 만화를 포함하여 대중문화 이미지를 활용하고 재구성하는 방식으로 작업하는 작가로 잘 알려져 있다. 그의 작업은 다큐멘터리 만화 작업, 그리고 '아톰'과 '미키마우스'를 접목한 '아토마우스(Atomaus)' 캐릭터 작업으로 크게 나뉜다. 1990년대 초반 다큐멘터리 만화 작업은 대중매체를 통해 자주 접하게 되는 대중문화 속 우상, 교통사고 현장, 범죄자 등의 이미지를 활용하여 만화처럼 묘사하는 방향으로 전개되었다. 1993년에 만들어진 '아토마우스' 캐릭터는 1994년 《리모트 컨트롤》에서 처음 발표되었다. 아토마우스는 역사 문화적, 지정학적 맥락을 담아내며, 다양한 형태로 끊임없이 등장했다. 이동기는 익숙한 기존의 시각 이미지를 통해 다층적인 맥락 속 그 의미의 발생과 변이를 들여다보고자 했다. 작가는 국립현대미술관의 《젊은 모색 '92》(1992)에 참여했으며 일민미술관 개인전 《크래쉬》(2003)를 비롯해 다수의 그룹전 및 개인전을 통해 작품을 발표해 오고 있다.

Lee Dongi (b. 1967) has chiefly produced paintings in which he selects and reconstructs images from comics and popular culture and transfers them to the canvas. His comic-based work can be divided into documentary cartoon work and work featuring his character "Atomaus." The documentary cartoon work began in the early 1990s with the artist painting single canvases combining two opposing images. Over time, this led him to create other works in which he frequently depicted images from popular media in cartoon form, including plane crashes and traffic accidents, popular idols, and wanted criminals. Atomaus was first created by the artist in 1993 and first presented at the 1994 event *Remote Control*. Atomaus constantly appeared in various forms, containing historical and cultural and geopolitical contexts. Lee wanted to look into the occurrence and variation of its meaning in a complex and multi-layered context with an existing visual popular image. Lee Dongi has presented his work at various solo and group exhibitions, including the *Young Korean Artists '92* (1992) at the MMCA and the solo exhibition *Crash* (2003) at the Ilmin Museum of Art.

남과 여
Man and Woman

1990

국립현대미술관 소장
MMCA collection

162×130.5cm(×2)

캔버스에 아크릴릭 물감
Acrylic paint on canvas

이동기의 초기 다큐멘터리 만화 작품 중 하나인
〈남과 여〉(1990)는 관습적으로 상반된 두 이미지와
단어를 각각 화면에 배치한 작업이다. 작가는 서로 다르다고
간주되는 개념과 이미지를 나란히 병치시켜 현상에 대한
이분법적 논리와 그 관습적 사고방식을 다루고자 했다.
이 작품에서 이동기는 미국 대중만화에 나올 법한 이미지와
기법으로 인물을 표현했다. 작가는 이미 충분히 대중적으로
널리 알려진 이미지를 가져와 작품을 제작했는데,
이를 통해 "아무것도 창조하지 않는 작가가 되고 싶으며,
창조하지 않는 것은 매우 자연스러운 일이다"라고 언급했다.

One of Lee Dongi's early documentary cartoon works,
Man and Woman (1990) is distinguished by being a
single canvas combining two opposing images and
words. In juxtaposing opposing concepts, the artist is
attempting to demonstrate the black-and-white logic
of contemporary individuals who view certain objects
and phenomena in simplistic "yes-or-no" terms. In this
work, he uses comic-book images and techniques
to show the figures. He has generally attempted to
eliminate aspects of the artist's subjectivity from his
work by drawing various frames from comics and
treating them as paintings. In reference to his objective
representation of well-known popular images on the
canvas, he has said, "I want to be an artist who does
not create anything; not creating is a very natural
thing."

이용백

LEE Yongbaek

이용백(1966-)은 홍익대학교에서 회화를 전공하고 1990년대 초중반 독일 슈투트가르트 국립조형 예술대학교에서 회화, 조각을 전공했다. 이후 비엔날레 등 다양한 국내외 미술행사에 초청받아 작품을 선보였으며 지금도 국내외 미술계에서 활발히 활동 중이다. 이용백은 인터랙션, 음향, 키네틱, 회화, 조각, 설치 퍼포먼스 등 모든 장르와 기법을 아우르는 작업으로 사회의 사회·정치·미학적 단면을 구체적으로 시각화한다. 특히 한국 특유의 사회·정치적 쟁점을 다양한 방법으로 관객에게 보여주며 문제점을 제시해왔다.

Graduating in Western painting from Hongik University in 1990, Lee Yongbaek (b. 1966) subsequently earned a degree in painting and sculpture under the Germany's State Academy of Fine Arts Stuttgart in 1990s. Since then, he has been invited to various art events such as the Biennale and is still active in domestic and abroad art circles. Lee concretely visualizes the social, political, and aesthetic aspects of societies through artwork that encompasses various genres and techniques, including video, installation, sound, interactive art, painting, and photography. In particular, his work addresses social and political issues specific to Korea and presents them to viewers in various ways.

기화되는 것들(포스트 아이엠에프)
Vaporized Things (Post IMF)

1999–2000

국립현대미술관 소장
MMCA collection

7분 19초
7 min. 19 sec.

단채널 영상, 컬러, 사운드
Single-channel video, color, sound

〈기화되는 것들(포스트 아이엠에프)〉(1999–2000)은 사회적 이슈에 대한 작가의 관심이 잘 반영된 초기작으로 1996년 독일 유학을 끝내고 귀국한 후 작가가 경험했던 IMF 외환위기를 담아낸 작품이다. 영상 속에는 서류 가방을 든 정장 차림의 남성이 산소 호흡기를 낀 채 물속을 힘겹게 걷고 있는 모습이 다각도로 담겨있다. IMF 외환위기 상황에서 "숨쉬기도 어렵다"라는 지인의 말에 영감을 얻은 이용백은, 수심이 10m 되는 물속에서 구조용 호흡기 하나에 의지한 채 힘겹게 버텨내는 모습을 표현했다. 물속에서 걷고 멈추기를 반복하는 남성은 결국 물속으로 사라진다. 생존을 위해 힘겹게 견디다 결국 기화되어 버리는 현대인의 삶, 그리고 1990년대 후반의 불안한 시대상을 보여주는 퍼포먼스 영상이다. 이 작품은 2002년 제5회 광주비엔날레에서 2채널 영상으로 상영되었다.

Vaporized Things (Post IMF) (1999–2000) is an early work by Lee Yongbaek in which the artist shows his interest in social issues. It depicts the devastating effects of the Asian Financial Crisis, which he experienced after returning to Korea from his studies in Germany in 1996. The video uses multiple angles to show a man in a suit as he staggers along using a respirator to breathe. The image of his walking with a rescue respirator while submerged in water reaching a depth of 10m was inspired by the words of an acquaintance, who described how it was "difficult to even breathe" at the time. He repeatedly stops and starts before finally disappearing into the water. This performance video represents the uncertain historical experience of the late 1990s, as well as the struggles of contemporary city residents who fight to survive within the standardized rectangle of social space, only to ultimately disappear. *Vaporized Things (Post IMF)* was presented at the 5th Gwangju Biennale in 2002.

서현석

SEO Hyunsuk

서현석(1965–)은 공간과 감각의 관계를 화두로 퍼포먼스, 영상 작업과 연구 활동을 하고 있다. ⟨헤테로토피아⟩(2010–2011), ⟨영혼매춘⟩(2011), ⟨매정하게도 가을바람⟩(요코하마, 2013), ⟨바다로부터⟩(도쿄, 2014), ⟨천사–유보된 제목⟩(남산예술센터, 2017), ⟨미완의 폐허⟩(김홍석 공동, 서울시립 북서울미술관, 2019) 등 관객의 감각을 전경화하는 장소 기반의 작품을 발표했다. 『미래 예술』(공저, 2016)과 『Horror to the Extreme』(공저, 2009)의 저자이자 다원예술 간행물 『옵.신』의 편집자이기도 하다. 현재 아시아 맥락에서 모더니즘 건축과 근대 국가 형성의 관계를 탐구하는 영상 작품을 시리즈로 만들고 있으며, 광주비엔날레(2011, 2018), 베니스건축비엔날레(2014, 2018), 시카고건축비엔날레(2015), DMZ국제다큐영화제(2019) 등에서 그 일부를 발표했다.

Seo Hyunsuk (b. 1965) have focused on the relationship between spaces and the senses via research activities, performances, and video work thematically. He has presented site-specific work that foregrounds the viewer's sensations, including *Heterotopia* (2010–2011), *The Divine Prostitution of the Soul* (2011), *Heartlessly Autumn Wind* (Yokohama, 2013), *From the Sea* (Tokyo, 2014), *The Angel – Tenuously Named* (Namsan Art Center, 2017), and *The Incomplete Ruins* (with Gim Hongsok, Buk-Seoul Museum of Art, 2019). Seo is also co-author of *Future Art* (2016) and *Horror to the Extreme* (2009) and editor of the multidisciplinary art publication *Ob.scene*. Currently, he has been producing series of video works exploring the relationship between modernist architecture and the formation of the modern state in the Asian context. Seo has shown some of these works at the Gwangju Biennale (2011, 2018), the Venice Biennale of Architecture (2014, 2018), the Chicago Architecture Biennial (2015), and the DMZ International Documentary Film Festival (2019).

"'Context' as a term
does not apply to Seoul"

〈잃어버린 항해〉(2011–2018)는 서울시 종로구 청계천로에 있는 세운상가(世運商街)의 역사를 다룬 다큐멘터리 영상으로, 여러 인물의 인터뷰를 중심으로 구성한 작품이다. 이 작품이 마무리된 2018년은 세운상가가 세워진 지 50주년 된 해이기도 하다. 세운상가는 건축가 김수근이 설계한 길이 약 1km의 주상 복합 건물인데, 건축가의 모더니즘적 이상과 당시 대통령이었던 박정희의 도시개발계획이 맞아떨어진 프로젝트였다. 작가는 이 도시개발 프로젝트와 관련된 사람들의 경험과 기억을 재구성하여 한국적 모더니즘의 의미를 추적해 보고, 미완의 유토피아와 그 파편들 속에서 또 다시 구축되어가는 다른 꿈들과 기대를 들여다본다. 이는 결국 우리나라 근현대사의 단면이기도 한 것이다.

The Lost Voyage (2011–2018) is a documentary that examines the history of the Sewoon Sangga, centering mainly on interviews with various individuals. The year 2018 marked both the conclusion of this work and the 50th anniversary of the Sewoon Sangga's construction. The Sewoon Sangga is a mixed-use residential/commercial building stretching for around a kilometer in length, based on a design by architect Kim Swoo Geun. It was a project that matched the architect's modernist ideals and the urban development aims of then-president Park Chunghee. The video uses interviews to reassemble the memories of people who participated in or were involved with the project. It reflects on the meaning of modernism in Korea and the distorted dreams that emerged from the ruins of a failed utopia. The landscape they create also provides a glimpse at aspects of Korea's modern and contemporary history.

잃어버린 항해
The Lost Voyage

2011–2018

국립현대미술관 소장
MMCA collection

단채널 영상, 컬러, 사운드
Single-channel video, color, sound

72분 26초
72 min. 26 sec.

최정화

CHOI Jeonghwa

최정화(1961–)는 우리나라 서민들의 일상에서 흔히 사용되는 소재이자 기물인 '플라스틱'을 자신의 창작활동에서 개념적으로나 조형적으로 탁월하게 활용하는 예술가로 잘 알려져 있다. 플라스틱 바구니라든지 양은 냄비 등 값싸고 흔한 생활용품들을 이용하여 특유의 재치 넘치는 설치작품을 선보이는 작가로 주목받았다. 작가는 홍익대학교 서양화과 졸업 후 이불, 고낙범 등과 함께한 《뮤지엄》(1987)을 비롯하여 《썬데이서울》(1990), 《쑈쑈쑈》(1992) 등 다수의 그룹전 활동을 했다. 1990년대 국내외 다수의 비엔날레에 초대되어 현대미술 작가로서의 입지를 확고하게 다졌다. 최정화는 미술 창작 이외에도 다양한 활동을 통해 자신의 작업 영역을 확장했는데, 대표적으로 '올로올로'(1990), '스페이스 오존'(1991)을 비롯해 '살바'(1996), '꿀'(2010) 등 복합문화예술공간을 기획·운영했다. 그는 미술 창작, 인테리어 디자인, 문화예술공간 운영, 출판, 아트 디렉팅 등으로 자신 스스로를 끊임없이 변모시키고 있다.

Choi Jeonghwa (b. 1961) is well known as an artist whose creative activities make superb conceptual and aesthetic use of plastic, an everyday material and item associated with ordinary Koreans' lives. He has drawn attention as an artist whose clever and distinctive installation work employs commonplace, inexpensive items such as plastic baskets and nickel silver pots. After graduating from the Department of Western painting at Hongik University, he participated in numerous group exhibitions, starting with *Museum* (1987) alongside Lee Bul and Kho Nakbeom, and continuing with *Sunday Seoul* (1990) and *Show Show Show* (1992). During the 1990s, he cemented his place as a contemporary artist with multiple invitations to biennials in Korea and other countries. Choi has also expanded his work to activities beyond artistic creation, including his establishment of various multipurpose culture and art spaces such as Ollo Ollo (1990), Space Ozone (1991), Salba (1996), and Kkul (2010). He is constantly transforming himself through his activities in artistic creation, interior design, culture space operation, publishing, art directing, and more.

최정화는 작업 초기부터 지금까지 지속적으로 '꽃'을 자신의 작업에 있어 주요 소재이자 주제로 다루고 있다. 난지도에 버려진 이불보의 거대한 꽃 형상 문양을 보면서 큰 충격을 받았던 작가는 이를 통해 삶과 죽음의 순환을 새삼 환기했다. 작가는 플라스틱을 비롯하여 다양한 재료를 가지고 꽃을 형상화하는 작업을 전개했는데, 거대한 크기와 화려한 색을 사용하여 제작한 꽃 작업 <슈퍼 플라워>(1995) 등이 잘 알려져 있다. <내일의 꽃>(2015)은 우리 생활공간에서 쉽게 볼 수 있는 인조 수목과 화분에 도료 코팅을 한 작업으로 철가루로 뒤덮인 시든 꽃들과 형광색으로 피어난 꽃들이 대조를 이룬다. 작가는 이 작품에서 살아있는 식물의 피고 지는 모습을 인조 식물로 표현하며 생과 사의 어김없는 이치를 거스를 수 없음을 담아내고 있다.

Flowers have been an important material and theme in artist Choi Jeonghwa's work ever since the earliest stages of his career. Profoundly struck by the sight of a large flower pattern emblazoning a discarded duvet on Seoul's Nanjido, he found that it evoked associations with the cycle of life and death. In his work, Choi had used plastic and other materials to represent flowers; well-known examples of this include his *Super Flower* (1995) and other flower-based works with immense sizes and brilliant colors. *Flowers of Tomorrow* (2015) stands in contrast to that with its flowers coated in powdered iron and fluorescent, blooming petals. Here, the artist has applied a coating of paint to the same sorts of artificial plants and flower pots that we might encounter around us. Through these, Choi represents the ways in which living plants bloom and fade and expresses how the relentless principles of life and death cannot be defied.

내일의 꽃
Flowers of Tomorrow

2015

국립현대미술관 소장
MMCA collection

섬유, FRP, 고무, 철분말 가루 혼합, 형광안료
Fiber, FRP, rubber, iron powder mixture
and fluorescent pigment

163.5×130×128, 220×203×188,
114×96×111, 161×120×104, 201×130×133,
230×114×128, 69×208×208,
132×130×129,
248×171×149, 230×147×156, 199×68×76,
155×60×35, 143×48×47cm

BACK TO THE FUT

Energizing Non-conformity

If "contemporaneity" is approached as something more than a mere temporal concept, as a matter connected with the problematization of existing hegemonic structures, a particularly good example illustrating this can be found in media-based artwork. The period between the late 1990s and early 2000s is often viewed as true blooming of Korean single-channel video works, because of the relations it bears to the historical context in terms of popular environment, video, and culture. In an age of media and video such as today, approaches such as non-linear narrative structure, segmented screens, temporal refraction, and skewing of visual and auditory sensations no longer seem strange. The late 1990s is perhaps the period in which this sort of vocabulary first became prevalent in artwork. This exhibition joins the viewer in observing the currents in Korean contemporary art, through the creations of contemporary artists who relate to disparate and complex temporal and spatial networks.

'동시대성'을 단순한 시간적 차원의 개념이 아니라 기존의 헤게모니 구조에 대한 문제 제기와 관련하여 다루어 볼 때, 이를 잘 설명할 수 있는 매체로 미디어 작업을 빼놓을 수 없다. 한국의 싱글 채널 비디오의 본격적인 개화 시기를 1990년대 말, 2000년대 초로 볼 수 있는 연유는 대중, 영상, 문화의 시대 맥락과도 맞닿아 있다. 비선형적 이야기 구조, 분절적 화면 전개, 시간적 굴절, 시청각적 감각의 뒤틀림 등은 지금과 같은 미디어 영상 시대에는 더 이상 낯설지 않으나 이 어법들이 작품에 본격적으로 드러나기 시작한 때는 1990년대 중후반으로 볼 수 있다. 이질적이고 복합적인 시공간의 관계망과 관련한 동시대 작가들의 작품들을 통해 한국 동시대 미술의 흐름을 들여다보고자 한다.

불일치의 활성화

박화영

PARK Hwayoung

박화영(1968–)은 미술을 전공하고 1992년 첫 개인전 《지구 위에 선 합법적 외계인》을 열었다. 이후 뉴욕에서 신조형 석사과정을 마치고 영화 제작 과정을 수료했다. 1995년 뉴욕 PS1 국제 스튜디오 프로그램 한국 대표 작가로 참여했다. 귀국 개인전 《먼지의 두께》를 1997년에 개최하고, 이후 뉴욕, 필라델피아, 도쿄, 오사카, 하치노헤, 난징, 암스테르담, 런던, 쾰른, 호놀룰루 등에서 초청 받아 국내외 전시 및 상영회에 참여했다. 작가는 비선형적 서사, 탈 장르적 연출 등을 시도하며 전시 외에도 영화, 출판, 인터넷 등 다양한 채널을 통해 작업을 선보여왔다. 1998년 싱가폴의 씨어터웍스가 주관하는 아시아 융합예술 워크숍 '플라잉 서커스 프로젝트'에 참여하고, 이어서 〈데스데모나〉 멀티미디어 공연에 비디오 아티스트 겸 퍼포머로 참여해 애들레이드, 뮌헨, 함부르크, 후쿠오카, 싱가포르 등에서 활약했다. 2000년대부터 미술, 영화, 공연 장르의 경계에서 작업하면서 2003년 개인전 《드라이브》와 2004년에는 공동 기획·제작한 〈컬트로보틱스〉 멀티미디어 공연의 막을 올렸다. 2007년 개인전 《치자와 단도》와 발맞추어 '책빵집' 독립 출판사를 설립해 아티스트북을 출판하기 시작했다. 2010년 복합미디어 개인전 《쿠바, 울트라소닉 블라인드 안테나》 이후, 2013년부터 '책빵집 온라인' 홈페이지에서 관객과 직접 소통하는 장을 모색하기 시작했다. 2019년에 독립영화 「아미마모미마모, 비너스 밴딧」을 제작하고 연출했다.

Park Hwayoung (b. 1968) majored in fine arts and held her first exhibition, titled *A Legal Alien on Earth*, in 1992. She went on to complete a master's program in new forms and study filmmaking in New York. In 1995, she took part as an artist representing Korea in the P.S.1 International Studio Program, also in New York. She returned to Korea and held the solo exhibition *Accumulation of Dust* in 1997. She has been based in Seoul ever since, earning invitations to take part in numerous exhibitions and screenings in cities such as New York, Philadelphia, Tokyo, Osaka, Hachinohe, Nanjing, Amsterdam, London, Cologne, and Honolulu. In addition to exhibitions, the artist has shown his work through various channels such as movies, publishing, and the Internet, attempting non-linear narratives and de-genre production. In 1998, she participated in the Flying Circus Project, an Asian multidisciplinary art workshop organized by the Singapore-based TheatreWorks. She went on to take part as a video artist/performer in the multimedia performance *Desdemona*, which has been presented in Adelaide, Munich, Hamburg, Fukuoka, and Singapore. Since the 2000s, Park has been working on the boundaries of art, film, and performance, as represented in her 2003 solo exhibition *Drive* and the 2004 multimedia performance *Cult-robotics*, which she co-planned and co-produced. Coinciding with her 2007 solo exhibition *Chija & Dando*, the launch of her independent publishing company Book Bakery enabled her to publish artist books. Following her multimedia solo exhibition *Cuba, Ultrasonic Blind Antenna* in 2010, she has been at work since 2013 exploring direct communication with viewers through the Book Bakery Online website. In 2019, she produced and directed the independent film *Amimamo Mimamo, Venus Bandit*.

〈소리〉(1998)는 떠돌이 개를 소재로 한 다큐멘터리 형식의 작업이다. 작가는 자신이 거주하던 아파트 단지 주변을 1년 동안 떠돌던 강아지를 사진으로 촬영하고 글과 드로잉으로 기록한 다음 이를 영상작업으로 연결했다. 수집한 파편적 자료들을 엮을 때 내레이션과 소리를 더했다. 영상 중간에 작가가 떠돌이 강아지와 교신하는 장면이 있는데 이 상황에서 마치 비밀코드와 같은 '소리'가 등장한다. 이는 서로 다른 언어를 구사하는 단절된 개체들 사이의 궁극의 교감을 향한 바람, 강아지와 작가 자신이라는 개체 간의 상호연관성, 유대감을 매개로 접근하려는 작가의 의도를 담고 있다. 개체로 살아갈 수밖에 없는 근원적 고독과 이를 공유하는 존재들에 관한 세미다큐멘터리(semi-documentary) 작업이다. 이 작품 외에 작가의 〈블러디 모나〉(2000), 〈별일 없지?〉(2002–2003) 등도 함께 소장되었다.

Jaywalker (1998) is a documentary work focusing on stray dogs. In photographs, writings, and drawings, artist Park Hwayoung recorded the life of a dog that wandered around her apartment complex for a year. She then connected these records into a video work. To produce her video, Park interwove her fragmentary materials and added narration and sound. Midway through, there is a scene in which the artist communicates with the stray dog. The sounds that appear here are like a secret code, expressing the artist's hope for some ultimate communion between disconnected individuals speaking different languages, as well as her intention of approaching the dog through the medium of interrelatedness and unity between two beings—herself and the dog. This semi-documentary work concerns itself with the fundamental solitude that is an inevitable part of life, and with the beings who share in it. Other works by Park in the MMCA collection include *Bloody Mona* (2000) and *Everything OK?* (2002–2003).

소리
Jaywalker

1998

국립현대미술관 소장
MMCA collection

15분 12초
15 min. 12 sec.

단채널 영상, 흑백, 사운드
Single-channel video, black and white,
sound

유비호

RYU Biho

유비호(1970–)는 한국 사회가 디지털 기술과 IT산업에 집중하던 시기인 2000년에 첫 개인전 《강철태양》을 발표하면서 작가로 이름을 알리게 된다. 유비호는 디지털 매체 기술을 최소한으로 사용하면서 아날로그 감성을 표현한다. 작가는 감각적인 이미지 위주의 표현보다 사회 권력 혹은 구조 앞에 유약한 개인을 보여주는 냉소적인 내용을 주로 담아내고, 기술적인 면을 강조하여 드러내기보다 동시대 인간사의 보편적이고 일상적인 이야기들의 복잡한 심리적 상황을 반영한다. 유비호는 《강철태양》 이후 작가, 기획자, 미디어 연구자들과 함께 예술과 사회, 그리고 미디어를 연구하는 모임인 '해킹을 통한 미술 행위'(2001)와 '파라사이트-텍티컬미디어 네트워크'(2004–2006) 등을 공동 조직하고 연구 활동을 이어왔다.

Ryu Biho (b. 1970) successfully established his reputation as an artist with his first solo exhibition *The Steel Sun* in 2000, a time when Korean society was heavily focused on digital technology and the IT industry. Ryu's work achieves an analog quality by its minimal use of digital media technology. He chiefly presents content in a cynical vein, focusing less on creating stimulating images than on showing frail individuals faced with the power and structures of society. Rather than emphasizing technological features, he focuses on the intricate psychological aspects of universal, everyday stories that are associated with contemporary people. After the exhibition *The Steel Sun*, Ryu joined other contemporary artists, programmers, and media researchers in co-organizing and conducting research through "art, society, and media research associations" such as Artistic Acts through Hacking (2001) and Parasite–Tactical Media Networks (2004–2006).

〈검은 질주〉(2000)는 1990년대 중반 이후 급속도로 퍼져나간 정보통신 네트워크가 초래한 빅브라더 시스템에 대한 불안을 영상으로 구현한 유비호의 초기 대표작이다. 1990년대 말에서 2000년대로 넘어가던 시기, 사회는 정보화를 통해 빠르게 전환되었고, 슈퍼컴퓨터, 인공지능, 해킹 등에 의해 개인 정보가 기업, 권력기관 등에 활용될 수 있다는 위기감이 점차 나타났다. 이 시기에 만들어진 〈검은 질주〉는 가상의 매트릭스(matrix) 공간에 여러 인물이 서로 자리바꿈하며, 어떤 통제·감시망에서 벗어나기 위해 탈주하는 모습을 3채널 영상으로 보여준다. 화면에는 모두 11명의 인물이 등장하는데 좌우에는 각각 3명, 중앙에는 5명이 끊임없이 질주를 감행한다. 끊임없이 달리기하는 인물들은 거친 숨을 내쉬기도 하고 발을 굴리면서 서로 모습을 바꾸는데, 인물들의 동작은 시차를 두고 반복되며 좌우대칭을 이뤄 정렬되어 있다.

Black Scud (2000) is a major early work by Ryu Biho which uses the video medium to depict the anxiety about "Big Brother" brought about by the pervasive role of networks in the rapidly advancing information society since the mid-1990s. In the year 2000, the transition towards an information society was moving ahead quickly, leading to growing concerns about the potential exploitation of personal information, tastes, and orientations by particular enterprises, power institutions, and individuals through the use of artificial intelligence (AI), supercomputers, and hacking techniques. Produced around this period, Black Scud is a three-channel video that shows multiple characters switching places in a virtual "matrix" space, as they attempt to escape Big Brother's surveillance network. On the three screens, a total of 11 people appear, with three each emerging on the left and right and five at the center to perform their endless "black scud." They constantly switch places, running and exhaling roughly while rolling their feet. Their movements repeat at intervals, arranged in left-right symmetry.

검은 질주
Black Scud

2000

국립현대미술관 소장
MMCA collection

4분 3초
4 min. 3 sec.

3채널 영상, 컬러, 사운드
Three-channel video, color, sound

함양아

HAM Yangah

함양아(1968–)는 서울대학교에서 회화, 동대학원에서 미술이론을 공부한 후 뉴욕대학원에서 미디어아트를 전공했다. 이후 서울, 뉴욕, 암스테르담, 이스탄불 등을 오가며 영상뿐 아니라 조각, 설치, 오브제 등 다양한 매체를 실험적으로 설치하는 작업을 지속해오고 있다. 작가는 여러 지역에 거주하며 겪은 경험을 바탕으로 시스템 내에 존재하는 개인과 집단, 그리고 사회화된 자연에 대해 다루는데, 다큐멘터리 촬영, 편집 방식으로 차별화된 주제에 맞는 내러티브를 구성한다. 주요 개인전으로는 《함양아_정의되지 않은 파노라마 2.0》(대안공간 루프, 2019)와 《함양아: 형용사적 삶―넌센스 팩토리》 (아트선재센터, 2010)가 있으며, 다수의 국내외 비엔날레와 기획전에 초대되었다. 2004년 다음작가상과 2005년 한국문화예술위원회가 선정한 올해의 예술가상을 수상했으며, 2006년부터 2007년까지 암스테르담 라익스아카데미 레지던시에 참여했다.

Ham Yangah (b. 1968) pursued her undergraduate studies in painting and graduate studies in art theory at Seoul National University before going on to study media art at New York University. Since then, she has been based in locations such as Seoul, New York, Amsterdam, and Istanbul, producing artwork featuring experimental arrangements of different media, including video, sculpture, installations, and objects. Based on her experiences living in different regions, her work focuses on socialized nature and the individuals and groups that exist within the system. She incorporates narratives suited to her themes, distinguishing them through her methods of documentary filming and editing. Her major solo exhibitions have included *Yang Ah Ham: Undefined Panorama 2.0* (Alternative Space LOOP, 2019) and *Adjective Life in the Nonsense Factory* (Art Sonje Center, 2010). She has also been invited to show her work at numerous biennials and special exhibitions in Korea and abroad. She received the Daum Prize in 2004 and was selected Artist of the Year in 2005 by the Arts Council Korea. Between 2006 and 2007, she participated in a residency at the Rijksakademie in Amsterdam.

〈픽셔너리〉(2002–2003)는 함양아의 작업이 감각 위주에서 서사로 옮겨가기 시작한 첫 번째 작품으로, 장소 이동에 따라 특정한 사건과 사람을 우연히 만나면서 서사를 전개해 나간 〈드림…인 라이프〉 연작 중 하나에 속한다. 〈픽셔너리〉는 작가가 독립영화 미술감독으로 일하면서 만든 영상인데, 예술영화를 지향하는 감독과 그의 스태프들의 영화 제작 과정에 대한 작가의 기록에서 출발했다. 영상에는 2개의 세계가 공존하는데, 하나는 독립영화 감독이 만들어내는 허구의 세계이고, 다른 하나는 이를 위해 분투하는 스태프들의 현실 세계이다. 이 두 세계는 우측에서 좌측으로 흘러가는 분할된 장면들 속에서 중첩 구성되어 있다. 경비행기 조종사 역의 배우가 차가운 물에 빠져 허우적대다 비행기 파편 위에 앉아 추위에 떨고 있는 장면(허구 세계)과 이를 보다 실감 나게 하기 위해 물을 뿌리는 작업이라든지 그 외에 실제 현장의 긴장과 갈등 장면(현실 세계)이 교차 편집되다가 이내 하나의 촬영 앵글에 모두 등장한다. 작품 제목인 '픽셔너리'가 의미하듯이 이 영상은 허구 세계와 그것을 포함하는 실제 세계를 겹쳐놓은 일종의 다큐멘터리 픽션이다.

fiCtionaRy (2002–2003) is artist Ham Yangah's first work from a period when she was shifting her focus from senses to narrative. It is part of Dream . . . in Life, a series of documentary narrative videos in which she creates narratives based on chance encounters with events and people while moving between settings. fiCtionaRy, which Ham produced while working as an art director for an independent film, began as a daily record of the crew's production process in which the artist shared her artistic fantasies with an aspiring art film director. Two worlds coexist in the video: one is the fictional world that the independent film director is capturing, and the other is the real world of the film crew struggling to make it a reality. The two worlds are juxtaposed in partitioned scenes that flow from right to left. For instance, a scene in which an actor plays the role of a pilot whose light aircraft crashes into the water and struggles to climb onto the wreckage while shivering in the cold (fictional world) is intercut with images of the crew arguing or splashing water to film the sequence realistically (real world); eventually, everything appears within the same camera angle. As the title suggests, fiCtionaRy can be seen as an example of documentary fiction layering the fictional world with the real world that encompasses it.

픽셔너리
fiCtionaRy

2002–2003

국립현대미술관 소장
MMCA collection

4분 30초
4 min. 30 sec.

단채널 영상, 컬러, 사운드
Single-channel video, color, sound

김세진

KIM Sejin

김세진(1971–)은 미디어 아티스트이자 영상 제작 프로듀서로 서울에서 활동하고 있다. 서강대학교 영상대학원 영상미디어과에서 영화를 전공하고 영국의 슬레이드 미술대학(UCL)에서 미디어아트를 전공했다. 작가는 이미지를 해체·재구성하여 공감각적인 서사구조를 구성한다. 형식적으로는 시네마적 문법과 다큐멘터리의 사실적 기법을 적용하는데, 영화의 기초 원리를 이용한 키네틱 조각, 디지털 전자 사운드, 다양한 종류의 매체를 이용한 드로잉, 텍스트 등 여러 시각 매체를 활용한다. 작가에게 영상은 촬영, 편집, 음향 등의 요소를 이용해 감정의 질감을 전달하는데 탁월한 매체인 것이다. 《태양 아래 걷다》(송은아트스페이스, 2019), 《우연의 연대기》(미디어극장 아이공, 2015), 《Prizma Residency #1》(프리즈마 스페이스, 이스탄불, 2015) 등의 개인전을 열었으며, 갤러리 정미소에서 「불분명한 풍경」(2008)과 동숭시네마테크에서 「더 크로스」(1999) 상영 프로그램을 기획했다. 제4회 다음작가상(2006), 영국 블룸버그 뉴 컨템포러리(2011), 제16회 송은미술대상(2016) 등을 수상했다.

Kim Sejin (b. 1971) is media artist and filmmaker/producer based in Seoul. She pursued graduate studies in film in the Film and Media Department of Sogang University and studied media art at Slade School of Fine Art, University College London. In her art, she forms synesthetic narrative structures through deconstruction and reconstruction of images. In formal terms, she makes use of cinematic language and documentary realism techniques while employing a wide range of approaches such as kinetic sculpture (incorporating basic principles of cinema), digital electronic sound, drawings in various media, and texts. To Kim, video is a superlative medium for conveying textures of emotion through elements such as cinematography, editing, and sound. Her recent solo exhibitions include *Walk in the Sun* (SongEun Art Space, 2019), *The Chronology of Chance* (Media Theater iGong, 2015), and *Prizma Residency #1* (Prizmaspace, Istanbul, 2015). She also organized *Undefined Landscape* (Gallery Jungmiso, 2008) and the screening program *The Cross* (Dongsoong Cinematheque, 1999). She received the 4th Daum Prize in 2006, Bloomberg New Contemporaries recognition in 2011, and the 16th SongEun Art Award in 2016.

〈되돌려진 시간〉(1998)은 시간의 물리적 흐름에 역행하는 일상의 순간을 다루는 작품이다. 각각의 비디오 클립은 울기, 성냥 켜기, 그리기, 말하기, 머리 말리기, 먹기 등 일상적인 행위를 촬영한 후 리버스(reverse) 기법으로 재생한다. 마치 당시 음악 전문 케이블 채널 MTV적인 이미지를 연상시키는 이 작품에 대해 작가는 일종의 미디어적 실험이라고 언급했다. 그는 일상적 행위의 순간을 담은 영상을 거꾸로 돌렸을 때 나오는 낯선 감각적 내러티브를 통해 또 다른 차원의 이미지를 드러내 보이고자 했다. 업계를 선도하며 컴퓨터그래픽 활황을 이끈 비손텍(Bisontec)에서 일하며 익힌 다양한 최신의 영상 어법들을 활용한 작가의 이 작품은 이전 미술과는 다른 감각으로 당대를 드러내 보이는 대표적인 예라 할 수 있다.

Reverse (1998) is a work that examines everyday moments defying the physical flow of time. The various video clips show everyday actions (crying, lighting a match, drawing, speaking, drying hair, eating, and so forth) that have been filmed and then played back in reverse. Recalling the "MTV" images associated with the time of its making, the work has been described by Kim Sejin as a kind of "media experiment." Through the unfamiliar sensory narrative that emerges when scenes of everyday actions are played backwards, she has attempted to show a different dimension of images. Making use of the state-of-the-art video language that Kim learned while working at Bisontec (an industry leader and driving force in the use of computer graphics), the work can be seen as excellent example showing the contemporary era with a different sensibility from previous art.

되돌려진 시간
Reverse

1998

국립현대미술관 소장
MMCA collection

6채널 영상, 컬러/흑백, 사운드
Six-channel video,
color/black and white, sound

2분 20초, 2분 34초, 2분 48초, 2분 22초,
2분 14초, 2분 55초
2 min. 20 sec., 2 min. 34 sec., 2 min. 48 sec.,
2 min. 22 sec., 2 min. 14 sec., 2 min. 55 sec.

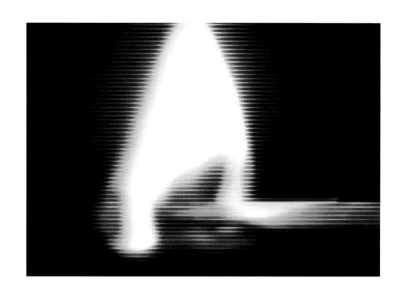

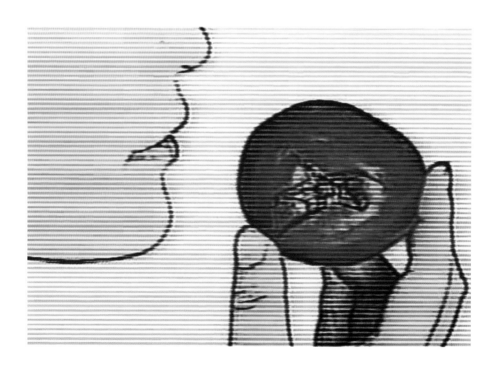

Hetero-geneity and Its Critical Time and Space

Korean society of the 1990s was marked by intersections and clashes between the benefits and drawbacks of the accelerated growth achieved through the rapid industrialization and modernization of the last few decades. Entering the postmodern era, while still facing issues that could not be resolved during the premodern and modern eras, Korea faced an environment in which different time frames were intermingled. Additionally, it was obliged to accept an untrammeled influx of globalization and neoliberalism. Among the artists encountered in this exhibition are some who grew up in and developed their creative capabilities during this period. These figures, whom we might refer to as "wholly contemporary" artists, were not confined by the conventional distinctions of genre or domain. They were quick to observe local and global trends of transformation, adept at strategically using newly developing economic and societal conditions and circumstances, and unhesitant about accepting their environment in terms of popular culture and society.

1990년대 우리 사회는 지난 시기의 급격한 산업화와 근대화를 통한 고도성장의 수혜와 폐해가 교차 충돌하고 있었다. 그리고 전근대와 근대가 해결하지 못한 난제들을 품은 상태에서 근대 '이후'를 맞이하여 서로 다른 시간이 혼재된 상황을 겪어야 했다. 이에 더해 세계화와 신자유주의의 거센 유입도 있었다. 이번 전시에는 이 시기를 관통하여 성장하며 창작 역량을 구축한 작가들이 포진해 있다. 그야말로 동시대 미술 작가라 명명할 수 있는 이들은 장르와 영역 사이의 관습적 구분에 갇히지 않고, 국내외 변화 흐름을 재빨리 간파하며, 다르게 전개된 환경을 거침없이 받아들이는 등 복잡다단한 현실의 관계망을 기꺼이 타고 넘나들었다.

이질성과 그 비평적 시공간

정재호

JUNG Jaeho

정재호(1971–)는 고도의 경제 발전과 성장, 그 이면의 사회 풍경에 주목하고 작업을 전개했다. 흔히 볼 수 있는 교회 십자가가 붉게 빛나는 서울의 야경, 화려한 불빛의 인천 차이나타운, 1960–1970년대 건설되어 지금은 철거 위기에 처한 시범아파트 단지 등은 작가의 핵심 소재이자 관심 대상이었다. 그는 근대화와 산업화를 통한 국가 발전과 이를 위한 정치·경제·사회·문화적 기제가 여전히 도시, 공간 속에 자리하고 있음을, 그리고 그 안에서 일상을 살아가는 우리 역시 의식적 차원에서 자유로울 수 없는 지점을 다루고 있다.

Jung Jaeho (b. 1971) focuses his artistic work on real-world landscapes representing the hidden aspects of accelerated state-directed economic development. His major interests have included nightscapes of Seoul lit up by red crosses atop churches; Incheon's Chinatown; and demonstration apartment complexes that were built during the 1960s and 1970s and now face imminent demolition. Jung's work observes how the forces of modernization-based national development and the political, social, and cultural mechanisms to achieve this can still be found in Korea's cities, spaces, and architecture—and how the consciousness of Koreans living with those environments can never be free from them.

작품 제목인 ⟨난장이의 공⟩(2018)은 한국의 산업화 시기 모습을 소재로 한 조세희의 소설 「난장이가 쏘아올린 작은 공」에서 따왔다. 고도의 경제 성장을 이뤘던 1970년대 일종의 유토피아적 공간으로 자리했던 복합생활공간인 세운상가에서 내려다본 서울 풍경을 보여주는 작품이다. 작품 속 상단 중앙에 떠 있는 '로켓' 하나는 사실적인 풍경을 어딘가 모르게 낯설게 만든다. 복잡다단한 서울 한가운데에서 거리와 시선을 달리하여 비행 물체에서 내려다봤을 법한 화면 속 풍경은 스산한 분위기에 생기마저 잃어버린 듯하다.

A Ball of Dwarf (2018) takes its title from Cho Sehee's novel *The Dwarf*, which focuses on Korea during its era of industrialization. It shows an image of Seoul as observed looking down from the Sewoon Sangga, a multi-purpose commercial complex that existed as a kind of utopian space during the 1970s, when Korea was undergoing rapid economic growth. The painting shows a rocket in the middle of the sky. The rocket has the effect of rendering this otherwise realistic landscape somehow unfamiliar. A vaguely lifeless and chilly mood is evoked by a landscape that might have been from a flying object, with a different distance and perspective compared with the busy Seoul city center.

난장이의 공
A Ball of Dwarf

2018

국립현대미술관 소장
MMCA collection

한지에 아크릴릭 물감
Acrylic paint on paper

400×444cm

금혜원

KEUM Hyewon

금혜원(1979–)은 사진 작업을 통해 현실의 이면을 탐색하는 작업을 꾸준히 전개해왔다. 특히 도시 풍경을 세심한 시선으로 바라보고 그 안에서 읽히는 또 다른 의미를 포착하고자 했다. 작가는 재개발 현장, 쓰레기 처리 시설 등 도시의 보이지 않는 움직임을 사진으로 기록했다. 재개발로 인해 생긴 도시의 흔적을 다룬 〈푸른 영토〉 시리즈로 개인전을 개최했고, 2013년에는 제12회 다음작가상을 수상했다.

Keum Hyewon (b. 1979) has shared various photography series in which she shows unfamiliar things hidden underneath the everyday surfaces of the city. She observes and photographs the often-overlooked movements in urban settings, such as the redevelopment of neighborhoods, the former landfill site of Nanjido Island, and an underground waste treatment facility. She held her first solo exhibition with the *Blue Territory* series, which focuses on the scars and gaps left behind by urban redevelopment. In 2013, she was awarded the 12th Daum Prize.

금혜원의 〈푸른 영토〉 시리즈는 도시의 재개발 공사 현장을 사진으로 기록한 작업이다. 작품에서 '푸른 영토'란 철거지역 내 침수를 방지하기 위해 덮어 놓은 푸른색 방수포를 의미한다. 작가는 이 푸른 영토야말로 재개발 논리에 의해 뒤로 밀려난 상황을 대변하는 것으로 보았다. 개발에 의해 얻게 될 수혜와 그로 인한 또 다른 폐해를 푸른색을 통해 표현해냈다. 그야말로 극사실적인 현장의 풍경은 형광빛이 돌 정도의 파란 방수천으로 인해 초현실적인 장면을 만듦으로써 묘한 혼돈과 이질성을 가져온다.

The *Blue Territory* series photographically captures landscapes concealed by blue waterproof sheeting in areas undergoing redevelopment. The "blue territory" in the title refers to places where blue tarpaulins have been used to prevent water infiltration in demolition areas. Keum Hyewon sees the image of tarp-covered redevelopment zones as symbolically illustrating the ways in which settings are eroded and territorialized by business interests. She views the blue of the tarpaulins as holding a dual positive and negative sense: hope for some, but pain for those who are being forced out. Using a surrealistic landscape with exaggerated blue tarpaulins, she ironically exposes the hidden aspects of the city obscured by these surfaces.

푸른영토-부유하는 섬
Blue Territory-Floating Islands

2007 (2019 인화)
2007 (printed 2019)

국립현대미술관 소장
MMCA collection

인화지에 디지털 피그먼트 프린트
Digital pigment print on paper

70×210cm

푸른영토 20
Blue Territory 20

2009 (2019 인화)
2009 (printed 2019)

국립현대미술관 소장
MMCA collection

인화지에 디지털 피그먼트 프린트
Digital pigment print on paper

70×210cm

백 투 더 퓨처

김상돈

KIM Sangdon

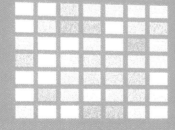

김상돈(1973–)은 베를린 국립예술대학교에서 순수미술을 전공했고, 공부를 마치고 2004년 귀국한 후 국내 여러 도시 풍경을 사진으로 기록한다든지 오브제를 채집하여 설치, 조각 작품으로 제작하는 등 다양한 매체를 이용해 사회 현실을 개념적으로 시각화해왔다. 그는 2009년 이후 사진과 영상, 조각을 하나로 설치한 〈장미의 섬〉, 〈불광동 토템〉, 〈솔베이지의 노래〉, 〈약수〉 등의 시리즈를 발표했으며 2011년에 에르메스 재단 미술상을 받았다.

Kim Sangdon (b. 1973) studied fine arts at the Berlin University of the Arts (Universität der Künste Berlin). Since returning to Korea in 2004, he has been using various media to conceptually visualize social reality. For instance, he photographs different urban landscapes in Korea and assembles objects to create installations and sculptures. From 2009, he has presented series such as *Rose Island*, *Bulgwang-dong Totem*, *Solveig's Song*, and *Healing Water*, which combine photography, video, and sculpture into single installations. He received the Hermès Foundation Missulsang in 2011.

〈모뉴먼트 제로〉는 종이와 유토로 조형물을 제작한 다음 이를 사진 촬영한 작품이다. 작가는 세월호 참사나 전국 방방곡곡 싱크홀 발생 등 무수히 발생하는 사건·사고를 보며 마치 "시공간에 구멍이 난 듯한 충격"을 받았다고 한다. 〈모뉴먼트 제로〉는 이처럼 사고로 사라진 존재들을 기리고 싶은 마음에서 비롯됐다.

Monument Zero is an artwork consisting of photographs taken of sculptures made with paper and oil clay. After witnessing the tragedy of the Sewol ferry sinking in April 2014 and sinkholes that emerged in various places throughout Korea, Kim experienced a profound shock, as though a hole had formed in time and space. To remember those who lost their lives in the tragedy, he created a "monument of absence" that he titled Monument Zero.

모뉴먼트 제로(서있는 사람, 안테나, 수미산,
일곱 개의 시간들)
*Monument Zero (Standing Man, Antenna,
Sumeru, 7 Kinds of Times)*

2014 (2019 인화)
2014 (printed 2019)

국립현대미술관 소장
MMCA collection

인화지에 디지털 잉크젯 프린트
Digital inkjet print on paper

44.5×29.7cm(×8)

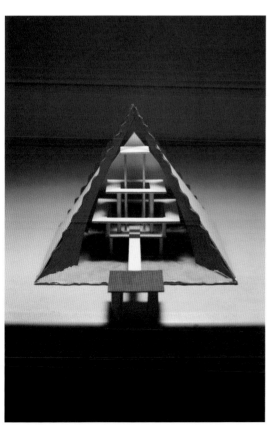

노충현

ROH Choonghyun

대학에서 회화를 전공한 노충현(1970–)은 정보통신 과학 기술의 발전에 따른 인터넷 환경의 전개와 2000년대 전후 급속히 확산한 디지털카메라 사용의 일상화와 맞물려 자신의 작업 속에서 회화와 사진의 관계를 탐구하며 풍경을 그렸다. 작가는 한강의 고수부지, 서울대공원, 테니스 코트나 수영장, 공터와 그 주변 풍경 등을 화폭에 담았다. 그는 본 것을 사진으로 촬영한 다음 이를 그림 그리는 데 활용했다. 작품 제작 과정에서 사진을 통한 기억은 대상과 현상에 대한 작가의 직접적 경험과 상호작용을 한다. 노충현이 오랜 기간 그린 한강과 그 주변 풍경 안에는 우리 시대, 사회, 도시 내 자리하고 있는 삶의 양가적 정서와 태도들이 담겨있다.

Roh Choonghyun (b. 1970) studied painting in university. Since the 2000s, he has created landscapes while exploring the relationship between photography and painting as digital cameras become increasingly ubiquitous. The scenes depicted on his canvases are a largely Parks in Hangang, Seoul Grand Park, tennis courts, swimming pools, open spaces, and its surroundings. Most of the work is empty with few characters, so it's more eye-catching. After capturing a scene in a photograph, he revises it until it resembles what he actually saw or believes himself to have seen. Yet in his painting process, the artist projects the psychological response that he personally felt in that setting. Roh's long-drawn Hangang River and its surrounding scenery contain the ambivalent emotions and attitudes of life in our times, society, and cities.

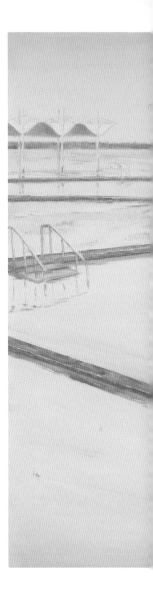

〈장마〉는 서울 한강공원을 그린 〈살풍경〉 연작 중 하나로, 2006년 여의도 한강공원 수영장을 촬영한 사진을 바탕으로 풍경을 재구성한 작품이다. 보잘것없이 메마르고 스산한 풍경을 뜻하는 '살풍경'이란 단어와 같이, 화면 속의 인적 없는 수영장 모습은 비 오는 날의 황량한 한강공원의 분위기를 더욱더 쓸쓸하게 만든다. 작가는 화면을 가로지르는 수영장의 경계선을 따라 하단의 로프에서 수영장 계단과 안전요원용 의자, 그늘 천막 등을 배치했다. 그는 이 작품이 애초의 사진과 달리 "부정확한 투시로 장소를 포착하면서, 되도록 물감을 얇게 발라서 뿌연 흙탕물의 인상을 포착하고자 했다."라고 설명했다.

Rainy Season is one of the series of Prosaic Landscape, which depicts the Parks in Hangang, and is a reconstruction of the landscape based on a photo taken of the swimming pool of the Parks in Hangang in Yeouido in 2006. The title Prosaic Landscape indicates that the landscape in question is dreary and insignificant; the image of the deserted pool on the canvas accentuates the bleak impression that the park along the Parks in Hangang conveys on this rainy day. Following the zigzag of the pool's edges across the canvas, Roh places ropes in the bottom, stairs, a lifeguard's chair, and a shade. The artist has explained that in contrast with the original photograph, he wanted to "capture the setting with an inaccurate perspective, applying the paint as thinly as possible to give the impression of a cloudy mud mixture."

장마
Rainy Season

2008

국립현대미술관 소장
MMCA collection

캔버스에 유화 물감
Oil paint on canvas

130×194cm

노재운

RHO Jaeoon

노재운(1971–)은 디지털 미디어 환경에서 인간의 시각적 경험과 인식, 그리고 사유의 문제에 대해서 웹 작업, 평면 그래픽, 사진, 비디오, 음악 등 다양한 매체를 활용해 탐구해 온 작가이다. 작가는 2000년에 '비말리키넷(vimalaki.net)'이라는 웹사이트를 개설하고 작업을 게시해 온라인 전시공간이자 일종의 웹무비 형식을 갖추었다. 이후 노재운의 작업세계는 미디어 환경과 삶의 가능성에 대한 관심으로 점차 확대되었다. 작가는 세계를 시청각 미디어인 영화적 장치로 인식하며, 우리의 경험과 기억 그리고 미래에 대해서 논의하고자 한다. 인사미술공간, 대안공간 풀, 갤러리 플랜트, 아뜰리에 에르메스 등에서 개인전을 가졌으며, 광주비엔날레(2006), 부산비엔날레(2012), 서울미디어시티비엔날레(2014) 등과 플라토미술관, 뉴뮤지엄 등 다수의 기획전에 참여했다.

Rho Jaeoon (b. 1971) is an artist who has explored issues of human visual experiences, perceptions, and thinking in digital media environments using web, 2D graphic, photography, video and music. He created a website called "vimalaki.net" in the year 2000 and uploaded his works to the site in the form of web movies. From there, his interests gradually broadened into matters related to media environments and the possibilities associated with life. Perceiving the world as one big cinematic device, he attempts to address people's experiences, memories, and futures within that. He has held solo exhibitions at Insa Art Space, Art Space Pool, and the Atelier Hermès and taken part in events such as the Gwangju Biennale (2006), Busan Biennale (2012), and Seoul Mediacity Biennale (2014), and as well as numerous feature exhibitions at the Plateau Museum in Seoul, the New Museum in New York, and elsewhere.

〈버려진〉(2009)은 웹아트 프로젝트로 발표된 작품으로, 작가의 웹사이트(god4saken.net)에서 1년 동안 상영되었다. 총 49개의 색면으로 구성된 화면에서 각각의 색면을 클릭하면 작가가 수집한 400여 개의 고전 느와르 영화에서 발췌한 특정 장면으로 연결된다. 영화 영상이 상영되는 중에 마우스를 클릭하면 색면으로 채워진 첫 화면으로 돌아가게 했기에 관객이 원하는 때에 영상을 재생하고 중지할 수 있다. 이것은 기존 영화의 관람 방식과 웹 무비의 경험을 구분 지어 보고자 한 작가의 의도가 담겨있다. 그는 영화의 한 장르인 '느와르'의 장면 중 암울한 분위기와 불안한 감정을 갖은 인물들의 모습에 주목했다. 느와르는 흔히 삭막하고 복잡한 대도시 공간(뉴욕, 홍콩)을 배경으로 하는데, 작가는 서울 역시 이러한 메트로폴리스적 도시라는 점에서 느와르를 미래의 서울과 연관하여 읽어냈다. 작품 속 49개의 색면으로 구성된 영상들은 두려움, 불안과 분열, 분노, 환상, 공포 등 현대인들의 심리와 정신을 반영한다.

As a web art project, *God4Saken* (2009) was screened for one year on a website (god4saken.net), which the artist developed. It consists of 49 color planes, which when clicked direct the viewer to film clips assembled by the artist from around 400 classic noir films. If the viewer clicks on the mouse while watching a clip, they are taken back to the start screen. In contrast with the usual approach to watching films, this allows the viewer to play and stop the clip at their discretion. Using this method, the artist aims to differentiate the web movie viewing experience from established film concepts. Selecting "film noir" as a cinematic genre, Rho focused on the characters as psychologically troubled figures in grim situations. Typically, noir films have been set in metropolitan urban settings (New York, Hong Kong, and so forth) that are highly artificial—in other words, places where nature has been conquered. As Seoul is becoming one of those metropolitan cities, the artist saw the noir genre as representing the future that awaits the city. The 49 short films in the work mainly depict mental/psychological aspects of human beings, including feelings of anxiety, division, anger, fantasy, dreaming, fear, and abnormal psychology.

버려진
God4Saken

2009

국립현대미술관 소장
MMCA collection

웹 베이스 아트, 컬러, 사운드
Web based art, color, sound

구동희

KOO Donghee

구동희(1974–)는 설치, 조각, 영상, 사진 이미지 등 다양한 매체를 활용하여 작업한다. 작가는 일상에서 발견되는 독특한 양상을 공간 설치와 영상으로 변형하여 현실에 드러나는 현상과 비가시적 세계의 3차원적 구조 이면의 진실을 보여준다. 최근 개인전으로는 ≪Flaget 2017–2117: 2022 Good Luck≫(쿤스탈 오르후스, 오르후스, 덴마크, 2022), ≪딜리버리≫(아트선재센터, 서울, 2019), ≪초월적 접근의 압도적인 기억들≫(페리지 갤러리, 서울, 2018) 등이 있다. 또한 부산비엔날레(부산, 한국, 2020), ≪Walking On The Fade Out Lines≫(록번드 미술관, 상하이, 중국, 2018), 제13회 샤르자 비엔날레 (샤르자, 아랍에미리트, 2017), ≪Embeddedness: Artist Films and Videos from Korea 1960s to Now≫(테이트 모던, 런던, 2015) 등 다양한 국내외 전시에서 작품을 선보여 왔다.

Koo Donghee (b. 1974) works with various media, including installation, sculpture, video, and photographic images. Koo Donghee captures unique aspects discovered in daily life, transforming them into spatial installations and moving images to show the truth beneath real-world phenomena and the three-dimensional structures of the invisible world. Her recent solo exhibitions include *Flaget 2017–2117: 2022 Good Luck* (Kunsthal Aarhus, Aarhus, Denmark, 2022), *Delivery* (Art Sonje Center, Seoul, 2019), *Overwhelming Memories of Transcendental Approach* (Perigee Gallery, Seoul, 2018). Koo has also participated in various international group exhibitions such as Busan Biennale 2020 (Busan, Korea, 2020), *Walking On The Fade Out Lines* (Rockbund Art Museum, Shanghai, China, 2018), the 13th Shajah Biennale (Sharjah, UAE, 2017), *Embeddedness: Artist Films and Videos from Korea 1960 to Now* (Tate Modern, London, 2015).

〈타가수분〉(2016)은 주점과 욕실이라는 각각의 장소에서 늘 있을 법한 활동인 요리와 목욕이라는 행위의 전 과정을 세세히 보여준다. 단골 위주로 오랫동안 운영되어온 작은 주점, 그리고 이 작품이 처음 상영된 로얄 갤러리 상설 전시장의 목욕 시설 세트에서 촬영되었는데, 이 두 공간은 거울로 사방이 둘러싸인 점과 TV 모니터가 배치되어 있다는 점에서 언뜻 비슷해 보인다. 하지만 각 공간의 기능적 측면에서 볼 때, 폐쇄적-개방적 구분이 서로 뒤바뀐 방식을 취하고 있다. 작가는 두 공간을 이어주는 이미지(강냉이, 거품, 동물, 계곡 등)를 중간중간 삽입하여 실제와 가상, 공간과 시간을 뒤엉키게 만들었다. 이러한 이미지의 교차 편집과 개입을 통해 서로 다른 시간, 상황, 공간이 상호 개입, 교신하는 바를 탐구했다.

CrossXPollination (2016) was filmed at a small, old pub that mainly serves a regular clientele and a bathtub set from an exhibition site for the Royal Gallery, where the video was first screened. The two quite narrow spaces appear outwardly similar, both being surrounded with mirrors reflecting in all directions and both with TV monitors positioned inside. But the artist's approach inverts the distinction of "closed" and "open" spaces in terms of their function. In detail, the work shows the entire processes of two actions that ordinarily take place in the pub and bathroom settings—namely, cooking and bathing. By interspersing these with images that connect the two spaces (corn, foam, animals, a valley), Koo creates entanglements of reality and fiction, space and time. Through the intercutting and intrusion of images, she explores how different times, situations and spaces mutually intervene and communicate.

타가수분
CrossXPollination

2016

국립현대미술관 소장
MMCA collection

단채널 영상, 컬러, 사운드
Single-channel video, color, sound

23분 58초
23 min. 58 sec.

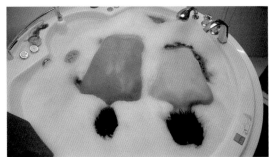

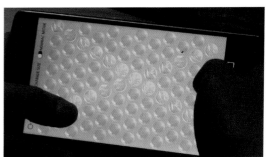

김두진

KIM Dujin

김두진(1973-)은 서울대학교 서양화과를 졸업하고 동 대학원을 수료했다. 작가는 대중문화나 포르노 같은 하위문화 속 상투적 이미지를, 또는 미술사 내 명화를 차용하여 성(性) 정체성과 이와 관련된 이데올로기를 다룬다. 작가는 3D 디지털 기법을 활용하여 주로 해골 이미지를 구현하는데, 해골은 인종이나 성별 등의 생물학적 표지가 사라진 이미지로 남근적 이성 중심주의 사고에 의문을 제기하고자 한다. 2018년 고양레지던시 14기 입주작가였으며, 《한국 비디오 아트 7090: 시간 이미지 장치》(국립현대미술관 과천, 2019), 《소란스러운, 뜨거운, 넘치는》(국립현대미술관 서울, 2015) 등에 초대되었다. 주요 해외전시로는 《베니스비엔날레 한국특별전》(2013), 한국현대미술 중남미 순회전 《박하사탕》(칠레산티아고현대미술관, 브라질상파울루현대미술관, 아르헨티나부에노스아이레스 국립미술관, 2007–2008) 등에 출품한 바 있다.

Kim Dujin (b. 1973) studied Western painting at Seoul National University and completed his graduate studies at the same institution. As an artist, he focuses on sexual identity and ideology, drawing on conventional imagery from popular culture (including live-action and animated films) and subcultures (including pornography) along with major works from art history. Since starting out in painting, he has chiefly created skeletal images using 3D digital techniques. As images lacking in biological indicators of gender or ethnicity, the skeletons show the artist's intent of resisting phallocentric thinking. Kim was a member of the 14th group of resident artists at the MMCA Residency Goyang in 2018, and he has recently been invited to present his work at the exhibitions *Korean Video Art from 1970s to 1990s: Time Image Apparatus* (MMCA Gwacheon, 2019) and *Uproarious, Heated, Inundated* (MMCA Seoul, 2015). His major overseas exhibitions include a special Korean exhibition at the 2013 Venice Biennale and the Central and South American touring exhibition of Korean contemporary art *Peppermint Candy* (Santiago Museum of Contemporary Art, São Paulo Museum of Modern Art, and the National Museum of Fine Arts in Buenos Aires, 2007–2008).

모세, 죽어가는 노예, 승리
Moses, Dying Slave, Victory

2016–2017

국립현대미술관 소장
MMCA collection

298×177cm(×3)

3D 모델링, 종이에 C-print
3D modeling, C-print on paper

<모세, 죽어가는 노예, 승리>(2016–2017)는 르네상스 미술의 대가 미켈란젤로의 조각 중 <모세>, <죽어가는 노예>, 그리고 <승리>의 이미지를 차용해 만든 디지털 회화이다. 3D 모델링 기법으로 동물의 뼈를 수없이 덧붙이는 방식으로 표현했다. 점토를 덧입히는 방식의 부조나 물감을 수없이 덧바르는 형식의 회화 기법을 디지털로 재해석한 것으로 볼 수 있다. 미켈란젤로의 조각은 성경과 신화 속 대상의 불멸, 영원성을 이야기하는 반면, 김두진의 디지털 회화 속 대상들은 죽음을 더욱 강렬하게 마주하도록 한다. 작가는 백인, 남성 예술가의 권력, 그리고 종교적 영향력을 언급하며 관습화되고 헤게모니적 우위를 점한 미의식에 물음을 던진다. 화면 속 무수히 많은 머리뼈, 뼈 조각들은 죽음을 상기시키며 이상적 아름다움의 인물상에 대한 이미지를 비틀어버린다. 이를 통해 당연하게 받아들였던 관습적 가치와 판단 잣대를 재고하도록 한다.

Moses, Dying Slave, Victory (2016–2017) is a digital painting that draws on the great Renaissance artist Michelangelo's statues of Moses, the Dying slave, and Victory. Employing 3D modeling techniques, the work is produced by assembling numerous bones from herbivorous animals. It represents a digital reinterpretation of the relief method with its application of clay or mud or the techniques of painting (with the application of numerous layers of pigments). Where Michelangelo's sculptures expressed the eternal nature of figures from the Bible and mythology, the subjects of Kim Dujin's digital painting are brought into even more powerful confrontation with death. Through his work, the artist is posing questions about the authority of white male artists and the aesthetic perceptions that have become customary and hegemonically dominant through the influence of religion. Signifying annihilation or death, the countless skulls and bone fragments that appear on the canvas have the effect of utterly breaking down the images of figures representing ideal beauty. The viewer is forced to reexamine conventional values and standards for judgment that have hitherto been taken for granted.

"Interfering with" or "Interventing in" the Future

Korean society has followed a very different trajectory from the pathways and temporal/spatial circumstances of the West, which moved linearly from the modern to the postmodern era and later from capitalism to late capitalism. From a context in which the premodern, modern, and (currently ongoing) postmodern overlap and condense, we see an unusual case of various situations and conditions existing as an "environment"—intermingled, constantly revised, and overlapping. In that sense, the contemporaneity of Korean contemporary art was established through the situational structure of hybridity and refracting from within Korea's specific spatial and temporal context. Ironically, the universal values of global contemporary that many artists pursued were in fact present within our autochthonic time and space.

우리 사회는 서구가 그랬듯이 모던 이후 탈모던, 자본주의 이후 후기 자본주의 등의 순차적으로 옮아가는 경로와 전혀 다르게, 지금도 끝나지 않은 전근대, 근대, 그리고 근대 이후가 중첩되고 응축된 상황 속에서 흔치 않게 여러 상황과 조건들이 뒤섞이고 거듭 고쳐지고 겹쳐진 '현장'으로 자리하고 있다. 이러한 점에서 한국 현대미술의 동시대성은 우리의 특수한 시공간 내 혼종과 굴절의 상황적 짜임을 통해서 확보된 것이라 하겠다. 그래서 우리 미술이 과거에 몹시 맞닿고 싶어 했던 세계 미술의 보편 가치가 지금 바로 우리 안에 자리하고 있음을 역설적으로 드러내는 것이다.

미래 간섭 혹은 미래 개입

김아영

KIM Ayoung

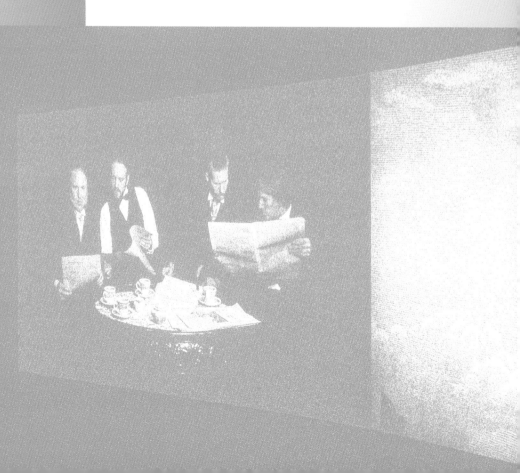

시각예술가이자 미디어 아티스트 김아영(1979–)은 경계와 세계를 넘나드는 주체와 사건, 중간적이거나 모호한 상태에 늘 관심을 가지며, 개연성이 부족한 세계의 속성을 반영하는 혼성적 이야기로 현실을 재구축해 왔다. 김아영은 생명정치와 국경 통제, 광물의 기억과 가상 메모리, 고대의 기원과 임박한 미래를 연결하며 광범위한 사변의 결과물들을 합성한다. 지정학, 신화의 파편, 테크놀로지, 미래적 도상을 종횡하여 혼합하고, 사변적 시간을 소급하여 현재 속으로 침투시킨다. 이는 영상, 무빙 이미지, 소닉 픽션, VR, 게임 시뮬레이션, 다이어그램, 텍스트 등으로 구현된 후 전시, 퍼포먼스, 공연, 출판의 형태로 노출되어 왔다. 갤러리 현대(서울, 한국, 2022), 관두미술관(타이페이, 타이완, 2022), 비데오브라질(상파울루, 브라질, 2021), 일민미술관(서울, 한국, 2018), 팔레드도쿄(파리, 프랑스, 2016) 등에서 개인전을 열었다. 샤르자 비엔날레(2023), 로테르담 영화제(2023), 아시안 아트 비엔날레(2021), 부산비엔날레(2020), 베를린국제영화제(2020), 《올해의 작가상》(국립현대미술관, 2019), 광주비엔날레(2018), 베니스 비엔날레(2015) 등에서의 단체전시와 스크리닝, 퍼포먼스에 참여했다. 프리 아르스 일렉트로니카 '골든 니카상'(2023), 춘천SF영화제 대상(2020), 올해의 작가상 후원작가(2019), 문화체육관광부 '오늘의 젊은 예술가상'(2015), 영국 로얄 아카데미 오브 아트에서 '브리티시 인스티튜션 어워드'(2010)를 수상했다.

In her multifaceted practice, media artist Kim Ayoung (b.1979) synthesizes the outcomes of far-reaching speculation, establishing connections between biopolitics and border controls, the memories of stones and virtual memories, and ancestral origins and imminent futures. These narratives take the forms of video, moving image, VR, game simulation, sonic fiction, diagrams, and texts that the artist presents as exhibitions, screenings, performances, theatrical projects, and publications. Kim decisively integrates geopolitics, mythology, technology, and futuristic iconography in her work, and she retroactively seeks speculative time to infiltrate the present. Kim Ayoung has presented solo exhibitions and international projects at the Kuandu Museum of Fine Arts, Taipei, Taiwan (2022), Palais de Tokyo, Paris, France (2016) and National Museum of Modern and Contemporary Art, Seoul, Korea (2019) among others. The group shows, screenings and performances include Sharjah Biennial 15 (2023); International Film Festival Rotterdam (2023); Asian Art Biennial (2021); Busan Biennale (2020); Berlin International Film Festival (2020); *Korea Artist Prize* (MMCA, 2019); Gwangju Biennale (2018) and Venice Biennale (2015). Kim is a recipient of the Golden Nica Award, Prix Ars Electronica, Austria (2023) and the Young Artist of the Year Award presented by the Ministry of Culture, Korea (2015)

〈PH 익스프레스〉(2011)는 1885–1887년 영국군의 거문도 점령사건을 모티브로 제작한 2채널 영상 작품이다. 'PH'는 '포트 해밀턴(Port Hamilton)'의 약자로, 1845년 영국군이 거문도에 붙인 이름이다. 6년을 영국에서 지낸 작가는 영국을 비롯한 서유럽의 근대화에 관심을 가지게 되었고 세계적으로 확산된 이 근대화가 우리에게는 어떠한 영향을 미쳤는지 살펴보게 되었다. 작가가 우선적으로 주목했던 인물은 묄렌도르프(1847–1901)라는 독일 외교관이다. 당시 조선의 정사에 영향력이 컸던 리홍장(李鴻章)이 조선을 감시하기 위해 추천한 인물로 묄렌도르프는 3년간 조선에서 일하며 화폐개혁, 세관 설치 등에 상당한 영향을 미쳤다. 이 독일 외교관이 국내에 머물던 당시 거문도에 파견되어 관여한 사건이 거문도 점령사건이다. 이 작품에는 영국 외교관, 귀족, 함장, 선원 등이 등장하는데 희극의 요소를 통해 거문도를 바라보는 이들의 다양한 시각을 담아내고 있다.

PH Express (2011) focuses on the historical event known as the Geomundo Island Incident (Port Hamilton Incident, 1885–1887). The "PH" represents the initials of Port Hamilton, which was the name given to Geomundo Island by England in 1845. Kim Ayoung lived in the United Kingdom for six years, during which time she developed an interest in the modernization process in the UK and Western Europe. She began to investigate how that modernization expanded at the global level and what effects that had on Korea. The first historical figure she focused on was Paul Georg von Möllendorff (1847–1901), a German diplomat who worked in Joseon's royal court. Li Hongzhang, a Qing Dynasty governor-general who controlled affairs in Korea at the time, recommended von Möllendorff to the court as a way of monitoring the Joseon government. While von Möllendorff only spent three years in Korea, he left a considerable mark with measures such as currency reforms and the establishment of a customs office. The Geomundo Island Incident occurred when British soldiers were dispatched to the island during the time that von Möllendorff was in Korea. The video features a British diplomat, aristocrats, a warship captain, and crew members sharing different perspectives on Geomundo Island through elements of comedy.

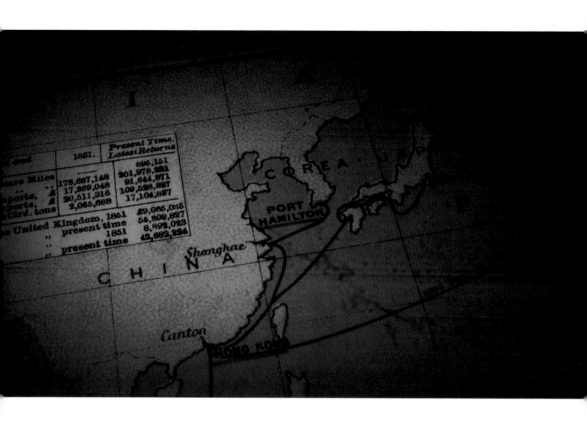

PH 익스프레스
PH Express

2011

국립현대미술관 소장
MMCA collection

32분 6초
32 min. 6 sec.

2채널 영상, 컬러, 사운드
Two-channel video, color, sound

Our Government would venture to sink a
million sterling into Port Hamilton.

the flagship Audacious,

Can we not take those wretched islands whenever we want them?

It appears to be a pleasant enough place

one of the officers bellowed out at the Russian captain,

unless Great Britain gave up Port Hamilton,
Russia will advance on Herat, Afghanistan.

But steam has revolutionised modern warfare.

They've chosen to leave the little cemetery

남화연

NAM Hwayeon

남화연(1979–)은 리서치가 촉발할 수 있는 수행성과 부재를 전제로 삼는 코레오그래피의 존재론적 모순에 주목해왔다. 이를 기반으로 시간의 불가해한 속성과 그것에 대한 일시적 개입, 존재와 실재의 취약함과 분화적 잠재성에 지속적인 관심을 쏟고 있다. 《가브리엘》(아뜰리에 에르메스, 서울, 2022), 《시간의 기술》(아르코미술관, 서울, 2015), 《앱도미날 루츠》(쿤스트할오르후스, 오르후스, 2019) 등의 개인전과 제56회 베니스비엔날레 본 전시(2015) 등에서는 인간과 자연, 역사 등 서로 다른 리듬과 주기를 경유하며, 기록된 시간이 현재에 새롭게 도래하는 사건으로 이행하는 현상에 대한 탐구를 보여주었다. 2012년 이래 근대 무용가 최승희(1911–1969)가 남긴 작품과 자료 등의 행적을 잇는 다년간의 리서치를 진행했으며, 이는 퍼포먼스와 퍼포먼스 아카이브의 관계 및 다성적 역사 쓰기로 확장되었다. 관련한 작업은 페스티벌 봄(2012), 제58회 베니스비엔날레 한국관(2019), 《마음의 흐름》(아트선재센터, 서울, 2020), 《Performance/Documentation/Presentation》 (룬드미술관, 룬드, 2020) 등에서 전시 및 공연되었다.

Nam Hwayeon (b.1979) has focused her attention on the exlstential contradictions of the choreography predicated on performativity and absence, which research can provoke. On this basis, she has directed ongoing attention to the inscrutable aspects of time and temporary intervention in them, as well as precariousness and differential potential of presence and existence. Through solo exhibitions such as *Gabriel* (Atelier Hermès, Seoul, 2022), *Time Mechanics* (Arko Art Center, Seoul, 2015) and *Abdominal Routes* (Kunsthal Aarhus, Aarhus, 2019) and group exhibitions like the 56th Venice Biennale (2015), she has presented her explorations of phenomena in which recorded time arrives in the present in new ways through different rhythms and cycles, including human beings, nature, and history. In 2012, she began a multi-year research project tracing the history of modern dancer Choi Seung-hee (1911–1969) and archival material on her work; this was subsequently broadened into an effort involving the writing of polyphonic histories and the relationship between performances and the performance archive. Related work has been presented at Festival Bo:m (2012), the Korean Pavilion at the 58th Venice Biennale (2019), *Mind Stream* (Art Sonje Center, Seoul, 2020), and *Performance/Documentation/Presentation* (Lunds Konsthall, Lund, 2020).

'약동하는 춤'은 1983년 개봉한 영화 「플래시댄스」 (Flash Dance)의 마지막 춤추는 장면을 북한식으로 번안한 '왕재산경음악단(王在山輕音樂團)' 무용의 명칭이다. 영화 속 여주인공의 전문 댄서로서의 성공 신화가 담긴 「플래시댄스」는 북한의 이데올로기와 이어지면서 집단 군무로 바뀐다. 개인의 성공이 최고 가치인 자본주의의 춤, 그리고 여성 신체에 대한 시각적 소비를 보여주는 미국식 춤은 북한에 유입되어 사회주의 집단 이데올로기를 선전하는 군무로 바뀐다. 작가는 문화번역 과정에 주목하고 이 춤을 2000년대 남한의 맥락으로 다시 끌어들인다. 작가는 안무가와 무용가 등과의 협업을 통해 '약동'이라는 용어를 토대로 '플래시댄스(일명 약동하는 춤)'의 움직임을 자세히 분석한 다음 새로운 움직임을 만들어냈다. 또한 유튜브 등에서 본 뮤직비디오 형식을 차용하여 새로운 춤으로 재창조했다. 1980년대 미국 춤은 북한의 이데올로기 댄스로, 그리고 2000년대 자신의 몸동작을 유튜브를 통해 유통하는 남한의 대표적인 대중문화 미디어 현상으로 다시 번안된다.

Throbbing Dance (2017) is an artwork that shows how the same gesture can be expressed differently in different contexts, including different eras and countries. The work takes its title from a dance by North Korea's Wangjaesan Light Music Band, adapting and transforming the dance performed by the protagonist at the end of the 1983 film *Flashdance*. While the original performance in *Flashdance* reflected an American woman seeking success as a professional dancer, as it became organically entangled with North Korean ideology, it ended up transformed into a group dance. In other words, an American style of dance—based on capitalist beliefs positing personal wealth and success as paramount values and involving the visual consumption of a woman's body—was imported into North Korea as a group dance that reinforced socialist collective ideology. By focusing on this process of cultural translation, Nam Hwayeon brings the dance into a South Korean context of the 2000s. Based on her collaborations with choreographers and dancers, she creates new movements based on her close analysis of the *Flashdance* performance, with a focus on the theme of "throbbing." The performance is also recreated in a way that draws on the format of music videos circulated over YouTube and other platforms. In this way, an American dance from the 1980s is translated first into a dance reflecting North Korean ideology—and then again into one of South Korea's representative media and cultural phenomena of the 2000s, where people circulate their own physical activity over YouTube.

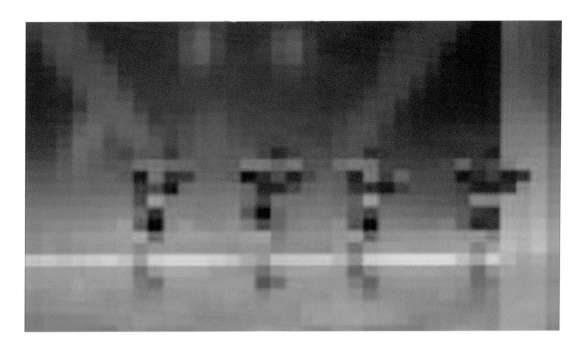

약동하는 춤
Throbbing Dance

2017

국립현대미술관 소장
MMCA collection

9분 19초
9 min. 19 sec.

3채널 영상, 컬러, 사운드
Three-channel video, color, sound

사진 제공: 오석근 Photo by Oh Sukkuhn

안정주

AN Jungju

대학에서 동양화를 전공하고, 대학원에서 커뮤니케이션학을 전공한 안정주(1979–)는 일상과 대중매체에서 이미지나 소리 등을 수집하고 이를 분절, 변형, 재조합하는 방식으로 영상 작업을 한다. 그는 개인 차원의 경험뿐만 아니라 사회적으로 공유하는 집단적 기억과 현상에 대한 다양한 이야기를 작품에 담아내고 있다. 제4회 후쿠오카 아시아미술 트리엔날레(2009), 제12회 광주비엔날레(2018) 등을 포함 다수의 국내외 전시에 참여했으며, 제5회 두산연강예술상(2014), 제17회 송은미술대상 우수상(2017)을 받았다.

An Jungju (b. 1979) majored in Oriental painting as an undergraduate and in communications as a graduate student. To produce his video work, he transforms, fragments, combines, and otherwise reconfigures images and sounds gathered from daily life and mass media. In particular, he shares a critical perspective on social and cultural phenomena and memories that are collectively shared beyond the level of individual experience. An has taken part in numerous exhibitions and residency programs both in Korea and abroad, including the 4th Fukuoka Asian Art Triennale in 2009 and the 12th Gwangju Biennale in 2018. He was honored with the 5th Doosan Artist Award in 2014 and finished as a runner-up in the 17th SongEun Art Award held in 2017.

〈영원한 친구와 손에 손잡고〉(2016)는 안정주가 스페인 바르셀로나의 한네프켄재단 레지던시 프로그램에 참여하고 이를 계기로 제작한 영상 작품이다. 작가는 자신의 유년기 향수를 불러일으키는 1988년 서울 올림픽, 1992년 바르셀로나 올림픽의 공식 주제가인 「손에 손잡고」와 「영원한 친구」(Amigos para Siempre)를 마치 하나의 곡처럼 리믹스하고 이를 중계 영상과 함께 편집했다. 올림픽 개막식 행사와 각종 경기 장면 중 일부는 원본과 다르게 재생 속도가 조작되는가 하면, 짧은 프레임으로 반복되면서 시청각적 균열을 만들었다. 이러한 효과는 아날로그 TV의 흐릿한 화면이라든지 노이즈 현상 등을 통해 더욱 증폭되는데, 세계화에 대한 시대적 열망을 의미하는 국가적 대형 행사와 그 이면에 자리했을 법한 갈등과 모순을 현재의 시각에서 환기토록 한다.

Hand in Hand with Amigos para Siempre (2016) is a video work that An Jungju produced while taking part in a Han Nefkens Foundation International Residency Programme in Barcelona. As the respective official theme songs of the 1988 Summer Olympics in Seoul and the 1992 Summer Olympics in Barcelona, *Hand in Hand* and *Amigos para Siempre* are two pieces of music that evoked feelings of childhood nostalgia in An. For this work, the artist has remixed them into a single piece, which is edited together with broadcast footage. The artwork evokes a sense of visual fracturing and tension by altering the speed and presentation of select scenes from the Olympics' opening event and competitions. The effect is amplified by the blurring and noise coming from the analog TV screen. The resulting performance recalls an international event that symbolized the yearning for globalization at the time— as well as revealing the conflicts and contradictions concealed beneath the surface.

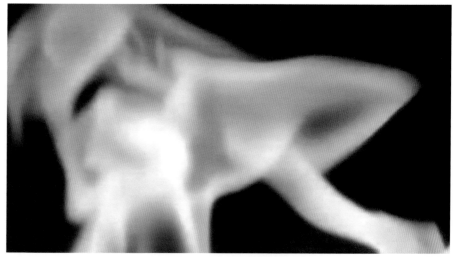

영원한 친구와 손에 손잡고
Hand in Hand with Amigos para Siempre

2016

국립현대미술관 소장
MMCA collection

16채널 영상, 컬러, 사운드
Sixteen-channel video, color, sound

8분 30초
8 min. 30 sec.

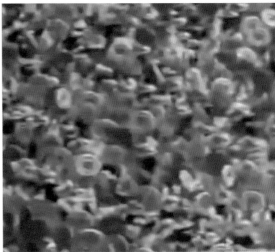

작품 목록 List of Works

공성훈
KONG Sunghun

79 블라인드 작업
Blind-Work
1992
블라인드 4개, 페인트, 알루미늄 테이프, 모터
Four blind curtains, paint, aluminium
tape, motor
100×100cm(×4)
국립현대미술관 소장
MMCA collection

81 버추얼 버추얼 리얼리티
Virtual Virtual Reality
1994
헬멧, 거울, 모터, 플렉시글라스
Helmet, mirror, motor, plexiglass
57×28×56cm
국립현대미술관 소장
MMCA collection

82 먼지 그림 (뒷산에서)
Dust Painting (at Mountain)
1996
캔버스에 먼지, 아크릴릭 물감
Dust and acrylic paint on canvas
181.8×227.3cm
국립현대미술관 소장
MMCA collection

84 개
A Dog
2001
캔버스에 유화 물감
Oil paint on canvas
112.3×145cm
국립현대미술관 소장
MMCA collection

87 개
A Dog
2001
캔버스에 유화 물감
Oil paint on canvas
130×162.2cm
국립현대미술관 소장
MMCA collection

88 모텔
Motel
2007
캔버스에 아크릴릭 물감
Acrylic paint on canvas
130.5×193.5cm
국립현대미술관 소장
MMCA collection

박이소
BAHC Yiso

93 역사의 문/역사적인 문
Entrance of History
1987
캔버스에 아크릴릭 물감
Acrylic paint on canvas
181.4×187cm
국립현대미술관 소장
MMCA collection

95 삼위일체
Trinity
1994
종이에 커피, 콜라, 간장을 섞은 용액
Mixed solution with coffee, cola and soy
sauce on paper
131×101cm
국립현대미술관 소장
MMCA collection

97 무제
Untitled
1994
나무, 아크릴 튜브, 간장, 야구방망이,
합성수지
Wood, acrylic tube, soy sauce, baseball
bat, synthetic resin
112×61×21cm
국립현대미술관 소장
MMCA collection

99 2010년 세계에서 가장 높은 건축물 1위–10위
World's Top Ten Tallest Structures in 2010
2003/2018, 2023
유토, 파이프, 알루미늄 좌대
Plastiline, pipe, aluminum table
130×180×80cm
국립현대미술관 소장
MMCA collection
작가가 남긴 드로잉 그리고 «박이소: 기록과
기억»(2018.7.26.–12.16., MMCA 과천)
설치를 바탕으로 재구성
Reconstructed based on the artist's
drawings and the installation *Bahc
Yiso; Memos and Memories* (July 26–
December 16, 2018, MMCA Gwacheon)

100 〈2010년 세계에서 가장 높은 건축물
1위–10위〉를 위한 드로잉
*Drawing for World's Top Ten Tallest
Structures in 2010*
2003
종이에 연필, 색연필
Pencil, colored pencil on paper
29.7×21cm
국립현대미술관 미술연구센터 소장, 이소사랑방 기증
MMCA Art Research Center Collection,
Gift of Yiso Sarangbang

김상돈
KIM Sangdon

180 모뉴먼트 제로(서있는 사람, 안테나, 수미산,
일곱 개의 시간들)
*Monument Zero (Standing Man, Antenna,
Sumeru, 7 Kinds of Times)*
2014 (2019 인화)
2014 (printed 2019)
인화지에 디지털 잉크젯 프린트
Digital inkjet print on paper
44.5×29.7cm(×8)
국립현대미술관 소장
MMCA collection

노충현
ROH Choonghyun

186 장마
Rainy Season
2008
캔버스에 유화 물감
Oil paint on canvas
130×194cm
국립현대미술관 소장
MMCA collection

노재운
RHO Jaeoon

191 버려진
God4Saken
2009
웹 베이스 아트, 컬러, 사운드
Web based art, color, sound
국립현대미술관 소장
MMCA collection

구동희
KOO Donghee

199 타가수분
CrossXPollination
2016
단채널 영상, 컬러, 사운드
Single-channel video, color, sound
23분 58초
23 min. 58 sec.
국립현대미술관 소장
MMCA collection

김두진
KIM Dujin

204 모세, 죽어가는 노예, 승리
Moses, Dying Slave, Victory
2016–2017
3D 모델링, 종이에 C-print
3D modeling, C-print on paper
298×177cm(×3)
국립현대미술관 소장
MMCA collection

김아영
KIM Ayoung

213 PH 익스프레스
PH Express
2011
2채널 영상, 컬러, 사운드
Two-channel video, color, sound
32분 6초
32 min. 6 sec.
국립현대미술관 소장
MMCA collection

남화연
NAM Hwayeon

219 약동하는 춤
Throbbing Dance
2017
3채널 영상, 컬러, 사운드
Three-channel video, color, sound
9분 19초
9 min. 19 sec.
국립현대미술관 소장
MMCA collection

안정주
AN Jungju

226 영원한 친구와 손에 손잡고
Hand in Hand with Amigos para Siempre
2016
16채널 영상, 컬러, 사운드
Sixteen-channel video, color, sound
8분 30초
8 min. 30 sec.
국립현대미술관 소장
MMCA collection

MMCA 소장품
특별전

백 투 더 퓨처

한국 현대미술의 동시대성 탐험기

2023.6.16. – 2024.5.26.
국립현대미술관 서울 1층, 1전시실 및 열린 공간

관장 직무대리
박종달

학예연구실장 직무대리
류지연

학예연구관
박수진

전시 기획
김형미

전시 진행
신기혜, 이솜이

공간 디자인
김소희, 홍예나

그래픽 디자인
김동수

공간 조성
윤해리

전시 운영
정재환, 서이정

소장품 관리
김은진, 강윤주, 이은지, 권혜은, 김유연, 김다은

소장품 촬영
김진현, 김국화

아카이브
박지혜, 양서윤

작품 보존
범대건, 이남이, 조인애, 윤보경, 임소정, 문희경, 송송이

미술관 교육
강지영, 김다연, 이슬기, 전상아, 정상연, 황호경, 김혜정, 선진아, 주하나, 윤지영, 최연진, 허진예

홍보·마케팅
이성희, 윤승연, 채지연, 김홍조, 김민주, 이민지, 기성미, 신나래, 이미지, 김보윤

고객 지원
이은수, 추헌철, 황보경

번역
서울 셀렉션

교정·교열
윤솔희

사진·영상
이미지 줌

목공
김건호, 프로날일러 목수팀

The Selected
MMCA Collection

Back to the Future

**AN EXPLORATION OF CONTEMPORANEITY
IN KOREAN CONTEMPORARY ART**

June 16, 2023 – May 26, 2024
Gallery 1 & Open Spaces, 1st Floor,
Seoul, MMCA

Acting Director
Park Jongdal

**Representative of Chief
Curator**
Liu Jienne

Senior Curator
Park Soojin

Curated by
Kim Hyoungmi

Coordinated by
Shin Kihye, Lee Somi

Space Design
Kim Sohee, Hong Yena

Graphic Design
Kim Dongsu

Space Construction
Yun Haeri

Technical Coordination
Jeong Jaehwan, Seo E Joung

Collection Management
Kim Eunjin, Kang Yunjoo,
Lee Eunji, Kwon Hyeeun,
Kim Yooyeon, Kim Da Eun

Collection Photography
Kim Jinhyeon, Kim Kukhwa

Archive
Park Jihye, Yang Seoyoon

Conservation
Beom Daegon, Lee Nami,
Cho Inae, Yoon Bokyung,
Lim Sojung, Moon Heekyoung,
Song Songyi

Museum Education
Kang Jiyoung, Kim Dayeon,
Lee Seulki, Jeon Sanga,
Jung Sangyeon, Hwang
Hokyung, Kim Heijeoung,
Sun Jina, Chu Hana,
Yoon Jeeyoung, Choe Yeonjin,
Heo Jinye

**Public Communication and
Marketing**
Lee Sunghee, Yun Tiffany,
Chae Jiyeon, Kim Hongjo,
Kim Minjoo, Lee Minjee,
Ki Sungmi, Shin Narae,
Lee Meejee, Kim Boyoon

Customer Service
Lee Eunsu, Chu Hunchul,
Hwang Bokyung

Translation
Seoul Selection

Revision
Solhee Yoon

Photos·Filmming
image Joom

Carpentry
guno, Team Pronaliler

백 투 더 퓨처

한국 현대미술의 동시대성 탐험기

Back to the Future

AN EXPLORATION OF CONTEMPORANEITY IN KOREAN CONTEMPORARY ART

발행인
박종달

제작 총괄
류지연, 박수진

편집
장래주, 류동현(페도라 프레스)

편집 지원
이솜이, 최혜미

번역
서울 셀렉션

교정·교열
윤솔희

사진·영상
이미지 줌

도록 디자인
강경탁(a-g-k.kr)

인쇄·제본
인타임

제작 진행
국립현대미술관 문화재단

초판 발행
2023년 8월 30일

본 출간물은 《백 투 더 퓨처: 한국 현대미술의 동시대성 탐험기》(MMCA 서울, 2023.6.16.–2024.5.26.)와 관련하여 발행되었습니다. 이 책에 실린 글과 사진 및 도판의 저작권은 국립현대미술관, 작가 및 해당 저자에게 있습니다. 저작권법에 의해 보호를 받는 저작물이므로 무단 전재, 복제, 변형, 송신을 금합니다.

©2023 국립현대미술관과 모든 저자들

ISBN
978-89-6303-365-5

값
28,000원

발행처
국립현대미술관
03062 서울시 종로구 삼청로 30

02 3701 9500
www.mmca.go.kr

Publisher
Park Jongdal

Managed by
Liu Jienne, Park Soojin

Edited by
Jang Raejoo,
Yu Tonghyun (Fedora Press)

Sub-edited by
Lee Somi, Choi Hyemi

Translation
Seoul Selection

Revision
Solhee Yoon

Photos·Filmming
image Joom

Design
Gyeongtak Kang (a-g-k.kr)

Printing & Binding
Intime

Published in association with
National Museum of Modern and Contemporary Art Foundation, Korea

First publishing date
August 30, 2023

This book is published on the occasion of *Back to the Future: An Exploration of Contemporaneity in Korean Contemporary Art* (MMCA Seoul, June 16, 2023 – May 26, 2024).
No part of this publication may be reproduced or transmitted in any form or by any means, electronic or mechanical, including photocopying, recording or any other information storage and retrieval system without prior permission in writing from prospective copyright holders.

© 2023 The authors and National Museum of Modern and Contemporary Art, Korea All right reserved.

ISBN
978-89-6303-365-5

Price
28,000 KRW

Published by
National Museum of Modern and Contemporary Art, Korea
30 Samcheong-ro, Jongno-gu, Seoul 03062, Korea

+ 82 2 3701 9500
www.mmca.go.kr